profitable

By
Kim Isaac Greenblatt

Kim Greenblatt Publisher
Published In West Hills, California

profitable
By Kim Isaac Greenblatt

Published by Kim Greenblatt,
West Hills, California, United States of America.

ISBN-13 978-1-60622-002-3
ISBN-10 1-60622-002-0
November 2008

This book is dedicated to my readers and anybody else who has stumbled upon, fumbled upon, dug, subscribed to my feed or liked my writing. Enjoy it and I hope it makes your life happier, healthier and of course, more profitable.

TABLE OF CONTENTS

Introduction

Welcome! This book is a collection of the first batch of my
blogs. Where appropriate, you will get additional commentary.
Some of my observations may stand the test of time, others
may be a time capsule of some pretty stupid things that I
might have written about. Some things that I nailed –
predictions of the economy adjusting downward. One thing I
didn't nail – Tropical Thunder doing well at the box office. Ah,
well. You hit some things, you miss some others.

The purpose of the blog is to talk about business, special
needs and at times, showing that talking about both things
doesn't have to be mutually exclusive.

I am not a financial expert. I am a father of two, a husband, a
businessman, consultant and tax professional who has been
dealing with money management and personal finance for
many years. I have managed projects, presented business
proposals to private industry and the government. The one
common thread that I find when I talk with people is that a lot
of them don't understand the need to deal with personal
finances.

I don't blame them. From early on in our lives we are
bombarded with spend, spend, and spend. If you watch
television or go on the Internet you are hit non-stop with
advertising. Listen to the radio? Sooner or later, no matter
how long the block of music goes, you are invited to spend
money on something or another.

We are in a different situation than our parents were in. Our
lives have gotten complex and we need to find ways to simplify
them so we can manage.

If you are caring for somebody with special needs or an elderly
person, you may find some items here to help you with

navigating the additional issues you might be dealing with food, clothing, shelter and personal considerations.

As with everything in life, you may only get one or two new pieces of information from this book. Generally, if the one or two items need can save you hundreds or thousands of dollars in the long run, you have made back the price of the book.

I am confident you will get something of value from the book.

For more information, please visit my blog, profitable, at http://www.kimgreenblatt.com/wordpress.

We'll get started now and I promise I will make it as painless and clear as possible!

Kim Isaac Greenblatt
October 23 2008

Things You Should Consider When Picking A Business
Thursday, July 17th, 2008

One of the biggest questions I get asked is, "Kim, what kind of business should I get into? What is the next 'big thing'?"

If I could predict the next big thing I wouldn't be consulting, doing taxes, writing, publishing, managing or coding. I would be doing the next 'big thing'.

The cliché answer is unless you really have an innate ability for correctly guessing the fickle public's taste, don't bother trying to guess what the public wants next unless you have a lot of money to burn. The number one thing you should be looking at is whether or not you like the business you are wanting to get into. It is a lot easier to do something you love than something you hate. Millions of people around the world are doing jobs just to get by. Here is a chance to do the one thing that you love.

You like to design rooms? If you think you can make a living with it in the market you are in, go for it. Bear in mind that you will have to figure out a business plan before you can actually start your business but make sure it is something that you love doing.

You may be pleasantly surprised that your business may turn into the next "big thing" and you will be there waiting to take advantage of it. The number two thing you should consider is what is your realistic income potential.

You may like to design rooms but if everybody else in Trenton, New Jersey or Ankara, Turkey is also interested in designing rooms the chances are that you will have a lot of people offering to design rooms for free. You will have a hard time paying the bills. Keep in mind that jobs (full or part-time) that are glamorous, exciting or fun have a lot of people wanting to do them. Competition is fierce and the market reflects the income you can potentially make accordingly.

If you are starting something brand new, or something yucky (cleaning out people's sewer lines), you will have less people (depending on the market in your area) in competition so you can forecast a better income stream.

Whatever you decide to do, take the time to make a business plan. A business plan is a blueprint for what you are planning to do. It should serve as a written document you can show others, potential bankers or people with money to invest (if you go that route) that you know what you are doing and know the direction that you will be going towards.

I will get into other things you should consider about picking a business to go into in the next post.

Questions? Comments? Please let me know.

Kim Greenblatt

Things You Should Consider When Picking A Business Part II
Friday, July 18th, 2008

Continuing on from where we left off from our previous entry, let's say that you've decided to do the job of your dreams. You really enjoy baking things at home. You think you would make a great baker. Maybe you love to fix things around the house. You've sat down and you have worked out that you think you could make a pretty good living doing this. The next question you need to ask yourself is, how easy is for me to get started in the business? This is called the ease of entry into the business or initial starting requirements.

You need to know or be able to research what the requirements are for doing business in the particular field that you want to work in. A good place to start is to strike up conversations with people who are doing what you are doing and don't live near your geographical location. If you want to be a plumber, for example, you may want to talk to one that isn't close to you so the person won't feel threatened. In the case of being a plumber, he (or she) probably won't feel threatened because there is a specific path of entry into being a plumber - you need to apprentice with an experienced plumber, take classes, etc.

This is the type of information you need to figure out before getting into your business. Do you have to have any specific licensing requirements for the city, county, state or national level in order to demonstrate competency for what you are planning on doing? You don't want a doctor who has had one year of junior college making a diagnosis on you and it is to be expected that different careers or businesses have different requirements.

If you don't have the requirements now, your mission is to determine what do you need to do to get the skills, how long will it take and will it be worth my while to go through the process to learn the skill or trade or get the street credentials that you might need.

That dovetails nicely into the next factor for consideration:

Is there a market demand for what you want to do?

You very well may want to be a plumber but if there are already ten plumbers in your area and there aren't a lot of people, there may not be a lot of work to go around. On the other hand in a large city like New York, Los Angeles, Chicago, Houston or Miami, you may not have to worry about finding work since there are enough people with broken sinks, toilets and water pipes to go around.

Here is where you take stock of your existing skill sets. If you have always been handy since you were a kid and have read up on how to change pipes, love working with pvc, and already have connections in the industry - you are on your way. The remaining aspect to this would be to demonstrate reliable work habits - are you on time for your jobs, are you honest, do you go the extra mile for your customers, things like that.

If on the other hand you hate working with your hands, hate getting dirty and have a fear of dirty water, maybe plumbing isn't the career choice for you.

More to come!

Kim Greenblatt

Things You Should Consider When Starting a Business III
Friday, July 18th, 2008

You've found a great job you want to do, you have the knowledge that you can make a living at the job, there is demand for your skills.

But is your job recession proof?

Are you doing something that withstand the swings that we sometimes encounter (like now for argument's sake) when people's checkbooks close and money is tight. Is the job or product or service you are providing something that people will still pay money for no matter what the economy is?

Consider starting a restaurant. When times are good, people eat out all the time. They would rather pay for the convenience of somebody cooking for them because they are all too tired from working. Let's face it, that is what microwave ovens are for as well. People are hungry and what instant gratification N-O-W.

What about when times are tough? The first thing that happens with most people is that they see what can they get rid of in terms of expenses. Where can they cut costs? For a lot of people that means shopping at the Dollar Tree stores and buying $1 meals. Cooking at home means they are saving money and the same goes for starting to bring a bag lunch to work instead of going out and spending anywhere from $7 to $15 for lunch like they use to.

If you are planning though on a business where you can sell inexpensive food, like a hot dog cart in a good location, you may have a recession proof business. Remember you still need to do your own due diligence and planning.

Questions or comments? Please let me know.

Kim Greenblatt

Things You Should Consider When Starting a Business IV-Start Up Costs and Overhead
Saturday, July 19th, 2008

In your business plan, you need to have what your start up costs are and what your monthly overhead will be for running the business. This would be a good time to also take inventory of your monthly personal expenses because if you are planning eventually on quitting your dayjob (or making this new gig your new day job) you should know how much you need to live each month.

Whatever numbers you come up with figure anywhere between 10-35% extra padding should be added to account for emergencies, holiday expenditures and if all things go well, money for expansion of your business.

Let's take the previously mentioned example of a hot dog cart. I have no idea if these numbers are realistic but they are here to serve as an illustration of start up costs:

hot dog cart	$3000
hot dogs	$200
buns	$200
condiments	$75
business license	$25
resale license	$0

fliers	$100
sodas and chips	$540
Total Start Up Costs:	$4140

and we will throw in 10% emergency cash of $414 to make our total start up costs a grand total of $4554.

Let's say you need to replenish the hot dogs, buns, sodas and chips each month. I know I forgot to add napkins so I can take some of that money from the emergency cash I allocated up front.

Our monthly overhead might include gasoline to drive to a location, say the front of the County Courthouse at lunch time - $300 a month.

Figure $1015 a month for expenses.

That is your monthly forecast for what you will need in the worse scenario cases if you don't even sell one hot dog. Are these acceptable costs for you and do you have the money to gut it out for 3-6 months till people see your cart and start realizing what a delicious hot dog really tastes like? What if the weather is lousy and you are stuck with rain for three months? How will you make expenses meet in the meantime since hot dogs won't keep forever and you will have to rebuy new ones?

Again, please be sure to do your research in advance and make sure that the startup costs aren't too high or that your expenses aren't going to mushroom out of control and eat up all the profits that you will be making!

Questions? Comments? Please let me know! Thanks for reading!

Kim Greenblatt

Things You Should Consider When Starting A Business V-Competition
Saturday, July 19th, 2008

Let's say that you have all the other elements for your imaginary hot dog cart business planned out. The next thing you need to take into account that should be incorporated into your business plan as well is your competition.

What are you up against in your anticipated marketplace? If you are selling hot dogs outside the city courthouse are there already three other hot dog vendors out there? Are all of them swamped at lunch and it looks like that if they had a dozen hot dog carts that they all would still be swamped?

Just because there is a lot of competition that doesn't mean that you should run away. On the contrary, that could mean that there is a huge demand for the product or service that you are trying to sell. You need to recognize though if the competition is seasonal or timely.

People won't eat dogs (usually) at 7 am in the morning if they are going to work at the courthouse. They might eat though between 11 am and 2 pm throughout the day. Maybe between 4-6 pm you might get another bump in business.

In the toy business, your seasonal sales in the United States are usually from October through December. In India, you can sell gold for weddings generally before monsoon season.

Are you also different enough from the competition to draw business to you from your competitors? Maybe you sell Kosher hot dogs. Maybe you have a cute girl in a bikini serving the hot dogs. What is your edge that will differentiate you or your product from your competition?

By recognizing your competition and incorporating it in your business plan, you show potential investors that you know what you are doing or at least have researched your market enough so that they can see that you are taking yourself seriously and will be treating your job as a business!

Questions? Comments? Thanks for reading!

Kim Greenblatt

Things You Should Consider Before Starting a Business VI-Time Commitment
Sunday, July 20th, 2008

Do you like to work long hours? Can you deal well with aggravation and stress? If you are planning on starting your own business you need to be able to deal with working ten to twelve hour work days initially. It will be your business and it will grow or wither away depending on how much time and energy you put in.

If we go back to our hot dog cart example, you can figure that you will move your cart from place to place to try and maximize the amount of hot dogs you can sell in an 8-12 hour period of time.

Let's say you need to open up your hot dog cart at the courthouse at 11 for the lunch hour rush. You are there for two hours so plan on getting an additional two hours of preparation each day to get to your first destination. From 2-4 you travel to some construction sites or to a stadium. From 4:30-6 pm you go back to the courthouse or stay at the stadium. Let us say that you move to an outdoor mall by the ocean to get the late night traffic. You end up staying there till 10 pm. You then take 1-2 hours to go home, clean up the cart and get ready for tomorrow's day.

Ask most independent businessmen and you will find that they work up 10-15 hour days easily. Most of them enjoy what they are doing so initially it isn't a problem.

But if you want to have a social life and get back to your family, girl friend, boy friend or relative of choice, you need for them to understand that initially they won't be seeing much of you because you are trying to start your own business.

Kim Greenblatt

Start Your Own Business or Buy An Existing One?
Monday, July 21st, 2008

If you are either out of work, caring for a person with special needs, or simply looking for a part time gig, one of the fundamental questions you need to ask yourself, is do you want to start your own business or buy an existing one?

Questions you need to answer are:

1. Do you want something already in place that had been established like a franchise with a proven track record or formula for success? If you have the net worth of several million dollars and want to open several of them, McDonald's franchises generally do well in recession and boom economies.

On the other hand, maybe you have your own recipe for burgers and fries and want to do it yourself from scratch to keep costs low.

2. Franchises are good if you want a blueprint for making a profit. For the better franchises, depending on marketing conditions, you can make a profit easier than starting something from scratch. On the other hand, you pay a hefty premium at times back to the company you are franchising from for the service.

If you have the business skills from running somebody else's business already, you can parlay them into your own job hopefully learning from your previous employer's mistakes.

3. If your goal is to make money, the larger franchises already have a track record for generating income. You can talk to people who own them and they can frankly tell you the nuts and bolts of what they like and what they don't like about

dealing with the parent company. In some cases it is the fees, in other cases there may be lack of marketing support or in even worse cases, the parent company may accidentally shoot the franchisee in the foot by offering the same product/service through a competing store.

Some supermarket chain stores were carrying Baskin and Robbins ice cream and that did not go well with people who were owning the franchised stores.

4. If you are an independent person who likes to handle things for him or herself, you could do well starting your business from scratch. The important thing is to still being able to listen to experts, competitors and the marketplace for making your decisions and trying to keep emotion out of the equation.

5. If you like to work within a system, you may be better off either buying a franchise or an existing store. The previous owner should share with you his or her secrets and recipes for success and being profitable. Just bear in mind that past performance doesn't always equate to future success, especially in the changing economy that we are all living through now.

Questions or comments? Please let me know!

Thanks!
Kim Greenblatt

Special Needs and Business
Monday, July 21st, 2008

A great market for people looking to start businesses is to cater to the special needs community. If you google "special needs" you will see there are all sorts of products, items for caring, devices to help to different types of blood testing, analysis, you name it, there is something out there for it.

That tells me that there is a large market for products for people with special needs or their caregivers. A great example is a portable pulley that can carry a person from a bed, to a table or chair, and then lift that person to into a tub or shower. As caregivers get older, they may not have the upper body strength to lift their charges - or themselves for that matter. Anything that can make caregivers lives easier and is relatively inexpensive can be a gold mine.

Rebuilding Gotham City, not such a profitable idea
Monday, July 21st, 2008

If you have seen the movie, "Batman, Dark Knight," you may have had the same questions that I did, at the end of the movie. Is it profitable to rebuild the city, or just call it a disaster area and have everybody move somewhere nice and safe, like Metropolis or Central City.

Spoiler Warning - PLEASE DON'T READ ANY FURTHER IF YOU HAVEN'T SEEN THE MOVIE YET!

Based on real life figures to build things, here is what I come up with (so far) for rebuilding Gotham City in terms of money.

Helicopter crash and building damage from Joker and subsequent side building damage and vehicle replacement for damaged vehicles in car chases for Harvey Dent- $28,000,000.

Lawsuit claims by victim's relatives - $13,000,000.

Remember, the Joker covered a lot of ground and did a lot of damage.

Rebuilding Gotham Hospital - $23,000,000.

Paying off insurance claims, lawsuits for victims of the Joker - $43,000,000.

Paying off families of the police officers who may or may not have been killed by Batman or the Joker or Two-Face - $18,000,000.

Bruce Wayne's insurance was cancelled from the last movie so he has to repair his own car - cost $190,000

Repairing Batmobile cost $13,000,000 - it is all custom work, remember.

Hush money to people who know his secret identity and cause him grief - one time lump payment of $3,000,000 for the people to keep their mouths shut.

At what point does the city find itself unable to get insurance? I seriously doubt that there is enough FEMA money to rebuild Gotham especially after repairing all the damage from the previous movie!

Did I miss anything? Post it in comments so I can add it!

Kim Greenblatt

No Job or Laid Off
Wednesday, July 23rd, 2008

No Job

You may have been laid off. Maybe you have quit an intolerable position. The important thing to do is to start working on a plan to get you back in some sort of position where you can get an income stream going.

First, if you have been recently laid off, take an inventory of what you have coming to you. Are you still getting some severance? Can you bridge your medical benefits over? Did you make sure that your retirement account, your 401K or pension plan is secure until you can take some time to decide what to do with it?

Make sure that they are not cashing out your 401K. If they are, make sure that you roll it over into an IRA – you will have generally up to 60 day to do it. If you don't it will be considered an early disbursement and you will be penalized and taxed.

If you have been laid off you will have to endure an exit interview. I wouldn't waste time saying what was wrong with the company, etc. You will need to use them as a reference. It doesn't pay to burn any bridges.

By the way, I wouldn't worry about any bad references. A lot of people are getting laid off and it is sadly pretty commonplace. Usually by law, a reference check will be that you worked for the company, were employed there for however many years and that is that. For personal references pick people you can trust – you don't want any nasty surprises when a prospective employer asks "Would you work with this person again?"
You also will be in a state of shock. Different people deal with stress differently but there will be some shock whether you are aware of it or not. It may hit you right away, it may not. However you react is normal.

If you start throwing things around the house and breaking your TV, that is not normal. Go for a walk or better yet run and get some of that anger out of your system.

If you need to contact a psychologist, counselor or there is one offered as part of your severance package – take the opportunity. It will help you get back on your feet faster.

Take an inventory of your financial assets and liabilities. If you have a financial savings that isn't in a retirement account, more power to you! You are ahead of most people. That means you have some time and leeway in trying to plan your next step.

If you can, file for your unemployment as soon as possible. The reason I say that is that it takes time for unemployment to process your application (they get a lot of them) and it may be several weeks till you get your first check. It doesn't hurt to get the ball rolling.

For the interim, if you have a family, plan on making some cut backs (if you can). Are there things you can start eliminating that you can always do later on?

For example, if you buy a lot of fast food, consider going to eat out only once or twice a week and load up on frozen food or fresh fruit and vegetables. I know that fast food sometimes seems cheaper and easier but in the long run it will only make you fatter and cost you money.

Buy coffee or tea to make at home instead of going to Starbucks. Start drinking generic sodas instead of Coke or Pepsi. Better yet cut out junk food altogether and get on a lean and mean diet for you and your family if you can.

Get your attitude focused on getting a new job. Personally, I don't like waiting to "get it together". If I know the direction I want to go, in this case, getting a new job, I start researching the internet, calling friends, calling relatives, doing whatever I can to get back employed. I have a family to feed. You may too!

If you have the luxury of time and money, you may want to use this as an opportunity to change careers. Make sure you understand though that the starting salary of your new career may be substantially lower than what you were use to making.

Make sure that it you have talked it over with your spouse, significant other or loved ones.   If it involves a significant lifestyle change for the whole family, they need to be in on it.

Speaking of lifestyle changes, do you have any services that you don't need while you are laid off? Maybe you need to cancel cable or satellite for a few weeks or months to save some money. Better to pay the rent or mortgage than to be watching the basketball game on satellite in the alley off of the street.

You want to try and get employed as soon as possible. Set some realistic time lines and if worse comes to worse, take some job – any job – that will start bringing some income in. I am not saying you should get a minimum wage job if it will end up exhausting you and you will still be losing money each month. I am saying that you need to be practical.

If you have been laid off for awhile – get your edge back! You need to get back to work and the longer you are sitting around the harder it is getting to get back to work.
Right?

So, you want to keep busy and avoid being lazy.

I would spend 8-10 hours a day working on resumes, calling companies, going to job fairs. Whatever it would take.

If you don't have web access, get it. Look for free web access (though I wouldn't send any personal information from a free site personally) at your local library, internet hot zones or neighbor's house (one you can trust). There are tons of ways to keep busy and you will need to write great cover letters and great resumes to get noticed in the crowd. I suggest you keep calling friends, head hunters, in fact, call stay in contact with whoever you think can help you land a job.

Start a website or a blog about what you are doing or what you want to do. Become an authority in your field and you will be pleasantly surprised.

If you hustle, your downtime between jobs will be small and you will be employed in no time.

Google job postings. As of the writing of this book, there are sites like dice, monster, and craigslist that have postings every day in all sorts of jobs.

Take advantage of this and dive in.

It will also keep you busy and sharp.

I keep thinking of when my wife Sharren and I would take Jacob (my son) on auditions for acting. You need to be ready and be prepared for a lot of rejection. Get a thick skin.

By the way keep your suit or dress pressed and ready. In case you get a call that you need to be at an interview right away – you can go in.

If you are over 50 (heck if you are over 35) and have gray hair, feel free to color it. Wear clothing that shows that you are the person ready to go to work and hit the ground running. This is a good idea regardless of whether you are a male or a female.

Show that you are a professional. Get to the interview early so they will see that you are responsible.

You will get the job. If not this one, the next one! Let us now move out of survival mode briefly into more practical money making ideas.

Profitable Exit Strategy
Thursday, July 24th, 2008

It is sometimes hard to have to think what your exit strategy should be in a business, especially if you are just starting out but in all good business plans it pays to know how you are planning leaving - either eventually by choice by selling off your shares of equity in the business or by necessity.

Part of a good exit strategy is to plan on how much do you want to retire on if you sell the business? The other way to look at it is, if my business looks like it is going under, how can I gracefully close the doors without screwing up my credit rating so I can open up another business later on?

The best way to keep on top of things is to have a place where you can contact all your creditors if you need to renegotiate contracts and payments. If you need to order product to continue to deal with a distributor, make sure you give the appropriate amount of notice time wise.

Back in the day when I was selling comic books through my comic book delivery service, Comic Cats, I saw that customers were starting to become delinquent with their payments to me. My profits at the time had dropped and I felt like I was the customer and my distributor was the wholesaler because things had gotten so expensive. I gave my two months notice with Diamond comics. Since I had to order comics two months in advance, I notified my customers who were subscribers, that I wouldn't be taking any more orders but I would complete their orders for the next two months.

Things worked out well and if I wanted to open a comic book shop again, my credit and reputation with them is (hopefully) intact. Remember that when you are leaving a business that you want to be able to recross any bridges that were built and it is hard to do if you have burnt them behind you!

Kim Greenblatt

Profitable Business Moves or Doing What People Hate To Do
Friday, July 25th, 2008

When people ask me, "Kim, what is one of the easiest ways to make money?" I have to tell them that there aren't any easy ways of making money short of inheriting it and leaving it to earn simple interest in a safe investment instrument. An easier way to make money though is finding what people hate to do and jumping into that market and doing it.

Take something simple like recycling. Back in the day, nobody wanted to haul or pick up trash. The savvy businessmen and companies that got involved in the trash hauling business discovered there was big money in contracts with other companies and even cities in disposing of garbage. The logical business after that was recycling. Getting people's garbage, sorting out what has monetary value and reselling it seems like a no-brainer during the green, ecological thinking times we are in now but the way to make money in that business is long gone. Simply put, the markets have already been mined, they are fiercely competitive and you would have to find places where it hasn't been worth somebody's business to start a trash collecting business.

The other major problem in finding businesses where people hate to have anything to do with them is that you have to make sure that there isn't a global competitor who can undercut you. Most people don't like to write computer code for example. You would think that computer programming would still pay decently and it does for some markets. If it is an up and coming computer system or product and people haven't jumped all over yet, you may have a couple of years of setting yourself up a decent practice with it. If you do good work and word gets around, you may be able to continue in the market despite saturation as more international outsourcing companies come on board to try and undercut you.

An interesting problem is that like all other products, even outsourcing gets to be expensive or not worth the aggravation if it ends up costing you clients or business. The reason some call centers are back stateside here in the U.S. is that some Americans still give good customer service over the web and phone and actually understand what your issues and concerns are.

So here is what I would do if I were young and looking for a great business move:

I would start looking at what are the junky jobs or things that people don't want to do and how much can I charge for me to do it? Is it also something I can physically (and psychologically) stomach doing even though I may be making money with it.

If you are a sewer electrician, you probably are working for utility companies or cities all the time. Not everybody is cut out for that work and it can be hazardous. Besides accidents happening underground, you can fall, get infection, possibly get electrocuted, well you get the idea.

Do you know why movie producers generally pay so little for new script writers, actors or actresses? It is because they know that there are thousands of people out there who will do that kind of work for free just to have exposure.

You will not find many people wanting to go down into a wet, cold and dark sewer to work on decaying electrical wiring and a rusted junction box for free.

Just remember in your planning to account for taxes and as usual, write your business plan down!

If you can think of any yucky jobs that people don't want to do, let me know. I know there is at least one TV show on cable about it and I suspect there will be more if nothing else just for the shock factor. For a lot of people they can live with the dirt and risk if the price is right.

The question is, is it also right for you?

Kim Greenblatt

You can be profitable or creative without spending money
Saturday, July 26th, 2008

After making a comment about saving some money, I realized that most business people (or at least the ones I've dealt with their taxes) spend too much money on things that don't need for their business.

Let me give you an example from back when I was starting up my comic book delivery business. I had saved money and was ready to buy a cash register for a swap meet, a credit card acceptance machine and the wiring for it, stock up an inventory of every comic book, poster and pog I could think of. After calming down and realizing that I would go broke in trying to get everything - not to mention to pay monthly fees for the credit card processing service AND a service charge for each transaction, I settled on the following:

1. Preorder of comic books of about $600 of merchandise, trading cards and posters at the retail level so my initial cost with a 50% discount (if it was that high) would be $300.
2. Licenses for selling comic books and working swap meets (my initial source of looking for clients who wanted me to deliver comic books to) - free.
3. Site fees to set up at each week at either Pierce College or the old Winnetka Drive-In swap meets - $10-20 a week for a table so in a month maybe $80.
4. A cash register - $250.

I mentioned this to a family friend and he said, "Why do you need a cash register? What's wrong with a metal box or even a cigar box?"

He was right! I ended up saving another $250 which I could turn into trading cards which I ended up selling.

I ended up getting clients from the swap meets. Unlike a lot of other people who had jumped into the comic book business to make money, I did not go broke from over-spending with my start-up costs.

In your business, do you really need a plush office? Is image important to what you are selling? If you are an attorney or in marketing, you might need something for potential clients to see that you are serious. You don't have to go overboard like some Century City attorneys use to and have marble flown in from Italy and placed in your building!

Think of ways to start up or continue your business that don't cost money. Be creative. There are plenty of one dollar, 99 cents and inexpensive stores where you can find goods to fill the gap that expensive stores sell. A lot of times the products are the same and you are just paying more for the name recognition from buying it from that particular store.

Little things like that may sound cheap but if you are starting up from scratch, trying to take care of a family of four, have a special needs daughter or any or all of the above, you want to make every penny count. It will pay off down the line as well because other business people will respect you for watching your money. Potential investors will see that you can be trusted with money and won't blow it all for things that won't help your business.

One last point. Nothing beats natural "word of mouth" advertising. The internet allows people to voice their opinion and tell you about goods and services. Sometimes some of the feedback systems can be manipulated but if you read between the lines, take the time to e-mail people or just ask your friends, you will see that honesty in business is rewarded with repeat business!

If you make a good product or offer a good service, people will come back (if they have the money). Not only is it a great and profitable idea (like the great and powerful Oz?), it will happen without you spending a cent (or euro, etc)!

For something that costs more than free, please check out one of my books from my site!

Kim Greenblatt

Profitable Marketing With Astrobase Go! It can be a tough venture, brothers
Monday, July 28th, 2008

For a clear example of how the unexpected can pop into your business, please check out this example of business in action from Astrobase Go! The Astrobase Go! team produce the popular television show, The Venture Brothers, on Cartoon Network's Adult Swim. They also do other video ventures. The Venture Brothers is basically a Johnny Quest/Hardy Boys

Grown Up and Grown Wrong series where the heroes are constantly failing. That has led to great success after a lot of work from the show's creator, <u>Jackson Publick </u>(a pseudonym of Christopher McCulloch). Doc Hammer is constantly left out, so major props to him for the hard work he puts into the show as well. At this point, major love to everybody else who works on the show!!!

Back to the marketing angle that you should take away to make yourself profitable...

I am not sure where they came up with this idea but it was pretty brilliant.

They would offer to sell a T-shirt a week to coincide with the release of each new episode of this season's Venture Brothers. If you preordered all the T-shirts for the series and prepaid, you would get a free shirt. I, as a fan of the series, took advantage of the offer. If you wanted to order one shirt at a time, you could and in fact as of this blog date, you still can. You just won't get the bonus shirt. I figure Astrobase Go! makes a decent mark-up on the T-shirts, the fans get nice shirts, the series gets extra marketing in the form of people walking around with their characters on their chests. There were some genuine, funny subliminal ads in the episodes such as the one where the Monarch decides he wants to buy a "Rusty Venture" souvenir shirt that suspiciously looks like one of the ones we will be receiving (please correct me people if I am wrong). It truly is a win-win situation for everybody. A profitable, marketing dream.

Except for the dreaded supply line problems.

Astrobase Go! has experienced what a lot of people in the comic book industry, book publishing industry or heck any industry have. They are not getting the shirts shipped to them from their manufacturers. To be fair, the gang at Astrobase Go! have stated that it will take 5 weeks till one receives the shirt. One shirt came out of sequence and that prompted an email reply from me. I am guessing I am not alone since there was a post on Jackson's blog that was pretty funny.

The shirts come in a white envelope scrunched down and that kind of made me wonder if they were sitting in the bottom of a mail bin somewhere waiting to get out.

The fact that I didn't get any more shirts for another week prompted another email. I am guessing they got a lot more emails from others as well again. The reply posted on his blog was pretty straightforward - a good business move. Customers will enjoy a good joke the first time they don't get something but the second time around they expect an answer with some sort of resolution. Apparently there are shipping problems, printing problems and they are being worked on.

Astrobase Go! has learned that when juggling a lot of things at once (and I should know since I burn the candle at both ends myself), it is tough to please people. I would suspect if they go for the shirt a week program for their next season that they will try to nail down a more reasonable supplier.

The takeaway from this as a business person is to try to get all your supply lines in place. There will always be problems and delays but you want to try and minimize them. Sometimes if you end up paying a little more for a little better service, everybody will be happy. I should also point out though that comic book, animation fans, fan boy geeks in general are a tough, motley lot to please and sometimes you can't do much about it.

In this case, I think Astrobase Go! is doing a great job. Go Team Venture!

Kim Greenblatt

Profitable Credit Planning For Business and Your Credit Rating

Monday, July 28th, 2008

If you are planning on starting a business, or running one already, you know that you may need extra money to start up or expand. That is where having credit comes in. Credit is basically where a bank, a credit card company or some lending institution (or person) gives you money with the promise that you will pay it back with a fixed interest rate.

The factors that creditors look for are similar and they boil down to the following (thanks to the Federal Government and the Consumer Handbook for Credit Protection Laws for the source of this information):
*
"What Creditors Look For
The Three Cs. Creditors look for an ability to repay debt and a willingness to do so–and sometimes for a little extra security to protect their loans. They speak of the three Cs of credit: capacity, character, and collateral.

Capacity. Can you repay the debt? Creditors ask for employment information: your occupation, how long you've worked, and how much you earn. They also want to know your expenses: how many dependents you have, whether you pay alimony or child support, and the amount of your other obligations.

Character. Will you repay the debt? Creditors will look at your credit history (see section on Credit Histories and Records): how much you owe, how often you borrow, whether you pay bills on time, and whether you live within your means. They also look for signs of stability: how long you've lived at your present address, whether you own or rent your home, and the length of your present employment.

Collateral. Is the creditor fully protected if you fail to repay? Creditors want to know what you may have that could be used to back up or secure your loan and other resources you have for repaying debt other than income, such as savings, investments, or property.

Creditors use different combinations of these facts to reach their decisions. Some set unusually high standards; others simply do not make certain kinds of loans. Creditors also use different rating systems. Some rely strictly on their own instinct and experience. Others use a "credit-scoring" or statistical system to predict whether you're a good credit risk. They assign a certain number of points to each of the various characteristics that have proved to be reliable signs that a borrower will repay. Then they rate you on this scale.

Different creditors may reach different conclusions based on the same set of facts. One may find you an acceptable risk, whereas another may deny you a loan."
*

Basically, you need to have your financial act together when you are applying for credit. The consumer handbook offers information and the protections that are out there but you need to show that you can be trusted with other people's money.

The weird thing is that the more you can be trusted and the more that you don't need the money, the more that the financial institutions will try to loan you - or at least that was the case prior to the meltdown in the housing markets.

It is also a good idea to watch how much credit you need and read very carefully what the terms are of the lines of credit, the loans, etc. You need to know what would happen if they call the loan due immediately. You need to know when and where to go into your credit.

If you are starting a business, make sure that you have this in your business plan. If you are already in business, make sure that you research carefully what you will need to have.

Kim Greenblatt

Profitable Gambling Advice-Don't Play the Lottery-the Odds Are That It Is A Sucker Bet

Tuesday, July 29th, 2008

Want some great gambling and investing advice? Don't play the Lottery. If you live in any state that has a state lottery, Powerball or any kind of bingo ball lottery, you've seen the ads, you've seen people become millionaires overnight. It doesn't happen very often.

In fact it happens so rarely that you have better odds of being hit by lightning, winning the Congressional medal of honor or winning the Nobel Prize than winning the lotteries.

They are built the way they are to make it seem that it is easy to pick numbers. How easy is it to pick numbers? Let's see from the California Lottery what the odds are...

How to Win California SuperLotto and Odds of Winning
To win you must have one of the following matches against the number actually drawn:

Match 5 Plus Mega (Jackpot Win!) Odds = 1:41,416,353
Match 5 (No Mega Match) Odds = 1:1,592,937
Match 4 Plus Mega Odds = 1:197,221
Match 4 (No Mega Match) Odds = 1:7,585
Match 3 Plus Mega Odds = 1:4,810
Match 3 (No Mega Match) Odds = 1:185
Match 2 Plus Mega Odds = 1:361
Match 1 Plus Mega Odds = 1:74
Match 0 Plus Mega Odds = 1:49
Overall Odds of a win is 1:23

Okay, so the starting payout is something like $7 million dollars? The odds of you winning are one out of 41 million? That doesn't sound like such a great deal. Yes, if you win, it is all worth it but realistically they should be paying you out $41,000,000. So, even if somebody wins out of the chute and they get $7,000,000, they have not paid out what the bet should have been worth.

What does that mean to you? If you really want to play or feel that your numbers are the lucky ones (and you may be better off going with random number Quick Picks to maximize your chances) you should wait till the jackpots are over $41 million. Otherwise, you aren't getting your bang for your buck.

Here is a profitable idea - how about taking each $1 that you want to invest in the lottery and place it in a savings account or donate it to charity each time you want to play the lottery? If you keep track of your donations over a year, two years or five years you will be pleasantly surprised at what your newly found savings or donations can do!

So, if you are also ready to see how your odds stack up, check out some of these comparisons:

Odds of going into a bowling alley and bowling a 300 game: 11,500 to 1

Odds of going to the golf course and getting a hole in one: 5,000 to 1

Odds of getting canonized: 20,000,000 to 1

Odds of being an astronaut: 13,200,000 to 1

Odds of winning an Olympic medal: 662,000 to 1

Odds of injury from fireworks: 19,556 to 1

Odds of injury from shaving: 6,585 to 1

Odds of injury from using a chain saw: 4,464 to 1

Odds of injury from mowing the lawn: 3,623 to 1

Odds of fatally slipping in bath or shower: 2,232 to 1

Odds of drowning in a bathtub: 685,000 to 1

Odds of being killed on a 5-mile bus trip: 500,000,000 to 1

So, your best deal is to save a dollar and don't take a bath while taking a 5 mile bus trip in a lightning storm while mowing your lawn with a chain saw!

Kim Greenblatt

Blogging Sucks and Is Boring, Like Most Bad Business Deals
Tuesday, July 29th, 2008

Besides catching your eye with this snappy posting title, most blogging does suck. It is very hard to monetize, most people don't really want to read that you woke up, took a shower, brushed your teeth, had breakfast, washed the dishes, blogged everything you just did, went to work, had a danish, blogged about it and wrote "I hate/love Obama/McCain and hate/love puppies." Some people just do it because they were told it is a way to socially network and get business.

Horsefeathers and poppycock!

The way you get traffic and readers, like I do for my books is to produce content that people find interesting (or at least amusing) on the web.

How does this relate to bad business deals you ask? Sometimes you are in a partnership that you are uncomfortable with because you are making money with it. Sometimes you are in a job you hate because you are making money from it. That is fine and the way of the world but you can do something about it like blogging. You can change what you are doing or at least start on the path to doing what you really want to do.

One client I had use to always complain when we met that she hated her business partner because she was always complaining. They never agreed on anything. I finally asked,

"Why don't you dissolve the partnership?" She said, "I'm making a lot of money and I am lazy."

Blogging is boring most of the time. Most business deals are pretty boring too. They spell out cut and dry what you are suppose to do and what the other party is suppose to do, what consideration is changing hands, how long will the deal last, and things like that. Both blogging and bad business deals have to be done because it is part of the process of well, doing business.

Eventually, most bloggers fall down and stop blogging or cut back their frequency because they have nothing to say anymore. Or they bored. The honeymoon is over.

The same is true with most jobs or businesses. You hit a wall and things get boring or downright yucky. Well, lucky reader, that is where giving the love comes in. If you want to blog or be a hit in business that is where you have to rise to the situation and start coming up with either:

1. New ideas
2. Greater Energy
3. Different Point-of-View
4. A Bit of Gratitude

There are no shortage of ideas or things to talk or write about. In fact, judging by the internet traffic that is out there, you can find anybody to talk about anything. Just write something and make it original!!!

You may be burnt out and just need some time to recharge. Fine, take it and return to business after a week or two.

You may need to look at things from a different perspective and that will help you with your business.

You also may have to thank your lucky stars that you aren't starving and as slow as things are, at least you have something going on.

It is true for business as much as blogging. We are going through in the United States a period of change and uncertainty. Money has gotten tighter but there is still money out there for investing and spending.

You just have to come up with the right combination of ideas, energy and perspective to get or keep something going that doesn't suck and isn't too boring.

If you put the excitement into what you are doing, others will find it exciting as well. Do what you can to turn around whatever business situation you are in to make it a win-win situation.

Kim Greenblatt

Profitable Or Practical Book Titles and Marketing and Recession Thinking
Wednesday, July 30th, 2008

I have completed the second draft of my next non-fiction book, tentatively entitled, "Practical Money Making-Surviving Recessions, Layoffs, Credit Problems, Generating Passive Income Streams, Working Full Time or Part Time and Retirement". It is not quite as long as the longest pop song title in the world, but it is up there in terms of number of words. When you are self-publishing, you are already swimming against the tide in the internet ocean. You are competing with book chains, their websites, other authors, other bloggers and apathy.

One of the best ways to get your book noticed is to make it unique. I've tried to do that with some of my other books on poker, on Rett Syndrome, tax preparation and dice and have had moderate success. This new book is going to be interesting because the title is going to be so long.

The theory behind it is that the book will be easily picked up by search engines when readers like yourself try to find out information on making money. As Morris Rosenthal had pointed out once, it is a lot easier to be found if you are in a unique enough niche but the problem is can you make a profit from writing a book in that niche?

Right now we are in state of flux. Some of the change is good and some of it isn't so good. There are a lot of people out in the United States who are losing their homes, their retirement, and don't know what to do. If they have special needs children or people that care in their house, it is even harder for them. I hope that my book will at least give them direction, some inspiration and some pointers as to what they might be able to do to help extract them from their situation.

The problem I run into as a underlined publisher, is that when it comes to money or savings or income, the internet is swollen with people trying to cash in on the words, pages or anything to get views. A lot of it is spam, get rich quick schemes. Some of it is legit and quite informative. As others have stated, you have to get creative to become a clear signal from all the noise that is generated from the internet.

I tell people who are trying to self publish to try and come up with something unique but accurately defines their book if they are trying to market it. There is a lot of information on trying to find key words that are easily searched. If you tend to go with these words the risk you run into is that you will be caught in the blizzard of spam and other people trying to cash in the same way you are. One of Kim's rules of being profitable is trying to do something different that the other person isn't doing. Even if it is only slightly different because the market is so large, it still pays to try to do something to give it your brand.

In hard times, people really want honesty as well as money. A lot of people feel disgusted because their investment brokers, their former employers and their government have betrayed their trust. It pays to be honest if you are writing non-fiction and that in itself should help generate word-of-mouth sales and buzz to sell your book.

For fiction, I suggest you put up samples of your work. Don't worry about people stealing your ideas. There isn't anything new under the sun and if you are worried, pay for a copyright before you post it. The only way that you will be discovered of creating the next Hobbit or Harry Potter or Dean Koontz book is for you to be out there. In keeping with my being brutally honest, fiction is A LOT harder to sell than non-fiction.

The reason is that fiction is very subjective in taste and what you find boring I might find exciting and original and vice versa. Nonfiction is basically the facts and straight information. People usually don't care who they get the information from.

Tying that back in from where we started, one way to stand out to shout "Hey I have the information you want at a moderate price" is to have a title that people can find or at the very least is unique.
The way I figure it, if they can't remember the title, remembering "Kim Greenblatt" might be easier.

Don't forget to post sample pages of your non-fiction on your website or blog. Listen to the feedback you get. Before you invest too heavily in your time and effort, make sure that there is a market - as well as an ungodly long name-for what you are trying to do!

Kim

Planning for A Disaster with Free Contingency Advice
Thursday, July 31st, 2008
You've gotten your business going and all is going well. What happens if you have an earthquake similar to the one that just hit California? How about if you have flooding like Louisiana, or parts of Asia? What about fires? As unlikely as it sounds, what about a terrorist attack?

If you don't have one, you need a solid contingency recovery or disaster plan. A contingency recovery plan is how to recover, keep the continuation of business and avoid a loss of your income stream. It can also be how you and your loved ones should react when you have a disaster. Having been trained in contingency planning, I have seen and been part of the implementation of a lot of systems. Talk about a lot of details! The gist of it is, it is better to be prepared and not have a disaster then not to be ready and something goes wrong. What could go wrong?

How about the 1992 Chicago Flood by the Chicago River? How about the World Trade Center terrorist attacks?

Remember that disasters don't have to be a catastrophe to be annoying. Smaller ones could be utility company failures, bad weather, or equipment just breaking down or failing. The reason that the Year 2000 programming bug (the fear that computer programs couldn't handle dates after the year 2000 accurately) was a non-event was that companies spent millions retrofitting, upgrading and reviewing their computer software and firmware to see if any date changes would cause any problems. If they had not done that, it probably wouldn't have been the end of the world however you can bet that a lot of companies would get a lot of complaints from their clients if their bank interest statements showed they owed interest calculated back to 1900 on their loans. The firms would have felt a lot worse if you came in with a bank statement showing that you were entitled to receive savings interest calculated from 1902!

Your contingency plan should be tailor made for specific actions you need to take if certain things happen. One a larger scale, certain levels of destruction have to occur before the Federal or state government support agencies are triggered into action. That explains why sometimes Governors, Presidents and the military are slow to offer aid.

You should have a contingency plan for your family as well. If you don't have one there is some free information further down in the article.

How do you begin in forming a plan?

First, get all the stakeholders together and decide what should be kept running or restored into operation if the business (or your family) gets disrupted.

What do you need in your disaster or contingency plan?

1. Establish a training plan and practice that you and your staff are safe and they are away from harm's way if something happens. Think fire drills, flood drills, earthquake drills.
2. Determine the extent of the damage and who to notify that there has been a disaster or problem (it could be as simple as the power going out in a thunderstorm and your backup generator has failed-don't laugh, it has happened).
3. Bring in the recovery team members to get the systems up and running.

If you are in a customer oriented sales business and have people in your store, make sure that you have an evacuation plan in place and test it periodically.

Do you have emergency lighting? Make sure that you have some way to see where you are going if the power goes out. Contrary to popular belief, it isn't the disaster that hurts people but things like people walking barefoot in cut glass or tripping in the dark afterwards.

If you can, take steps get what insurance coverages you need now. Once a minor event like a small flood happens, people start trying to get coverage and rates go up (if they haven't already with all the flooding going on worldwide in the last few years).

There are a lot of other issues to take into consideration and if you want specific information, check with the link below or post your questions in the comments section.

44

If nothing else, please take away information that you should have a contingency plan in place for you, your family and business if nothing else so that if all goes well, you will never ever have to use it.

For information about what to have for your own disaster planning, you might want to check out the free information at FEMA. They have some great stuff about planning there.

Kim Greenblatt

Federal Employer Identification Number or EIN

Friday, August 01, 2008, 4:18:13 PM | admin

To answer a question from my email (Fair warning, the post has been cannibalized from the IRS website and not all my ramblings):

As a business owner you may be required to get a Federal Employer Identification Number or EIN. The EIN identifies tax returns filed with the IRS. You have to get an EIN if you: pay wages to employees, have a self-employed retirement plan, operate your business as a corporation or partnership, or are required to file any of these tax returns, employment, excise, fiduciary, or alcohol, tobacco, and firearms.

If you're a sole proprietor with no employees and don't meet any of these requirements you don't need an EIN for dealing with the IRS. Still, you may need one for dealing with other businesses including banks that require an EIN to set up business accounts. If you ask for it, the IRS will give you an EIN even if you don't need it for IRS purposes.

The easiest and fastest way to get an EIN is online. If you go to irs.gov, search on the keyword EIN and complete the form, you'll get your EIN within minutes. Sorry for the short post but I am working on some other items that should hit the site in the next few days..
Kim Greenblatt

Kevin Rose is he an alcoholic, urine drinker or none of that?

Saturday, August 02, 2008, 12:06:31 PM | admin

Shamelessly picking on Kevin Rose for my own self-serving interests and to educate you guys and gals about critical thinking and gambling let me throw this out there. What is Kevin Rose drinking?

Seriously. He just had another announcement about another upgrade to Digg and there he is again with that blissed out grin of his holding a fluted glass with something in it. That, my friendly readers, is the question. What is it he is drinking? First blush, somebody would say that it is champagne. Okay, he has a great company and he is celebrating. I don't know him personally so I can't say if that is really Martinelli's apple cider. Same kinda bubbling. Maybe it is just water. Maybe it is something faintly bubbling like Fizzies.

Maybe it is urine. Yuch. To each his own I suppose.

Here is the deal. If I have done my job right, I have got you thinking about not taking images at face value. For all of us humans that have been thrown into forced short term attention span thinking, we look at an image and depending on our background and experience, make a logical conclusion based on our own experiences without thinking about asking the question - what exactly am I looking at?

Most of the time, you can pretty much assume that what you are looking at is what it seems to be. Whatever it is that Kevin Rose is drinking, he clearly is happy about it and is in either a toasting mood ("To urine?" Yuck) or to us ("To my Diggers" Better and not so Yuck). The impression that he wanted to deliver is clear and well received. Pretty innocent so far, huh?

The problem in real life is when you get news pieces, web blasts, pictures and information without anything other than a sound bite or web blast. Most people turn into parrots and start repeating what they have heard without thinking about was the context of the information. Questions you need to ask yourself or at least think about when you get information (and even from a guy who writes about urine like me) are:

What is the context of the information?
What does the person who is releasing the information have to gain from telling us about it?
Is it really from an unbiased source or am I being gamed?

With the coming political campaign hitting a head I strongly urge everybody to really listen to the candidates and ask them hard, clear questions that you are entitled to get hard, clear answers.

When you see the ads from either party, make sure you sift through the rhetoric, the emotional bullets they are trying to fire and get to the meat of the images.

The same holds true in business and in gambling. People will focus in on anything that will reinforce what they believe in. When it comes to craps for example, people think that just because a number hasn't been thrown with the dice that the number is "due". The reality is that the odds are the same for each throw of a pair of dice (if they are not fixed) no matter what.

When it comes to something more subjective like pictures, videos and articles (especially by urine writers like me), things aren't cut and dry. As you speed thru your digging or your social interactions of choice, please take the time to sometimes ask what is going on behind the scenes.

Oh, and by the way, for whoever gets to be elected President, if you want to get America going, spend money rebuilding the infrastructure (freeways, bridges, roadways, dams, etc). The money will be put to keeping America together in a very LITERAL sense, it will create jobs in America, and the people making that money will spend it in America.

Oh, and spend more money in helping people and families with special needs, like Rett Syndrome.

See? All of that urine stuff was just to get your attention to tell you how you should vote and what you should you tell your candidate of choice!

Hold'em Turn Rats As Bad As River Rats and Random Reinforcement

Saturday, August 02, 2008, 11:54:17 PM | admin

If you play Texas Hold'em, you have no doubt heard of the term, "River Rat". That is the unglamorous phrase used for people who by any stretch of the imagination should have folded their cards earlier but by sticking around and throwing in their money, they end up winning the hand.

You may have encountered "Turn Rats" in low limit no limit games or games where people want action:

You are in the big blind at a $40NL table. Players just come in and no raises. The stacks are all roughly the same. Here is our flop:

You bet $5 and everybody folds except one player who calls.

You   Your Opponent

You are the favorite here but since it is low limit, no fold'em $40 hold'em you aren't sure if this player is holding pocket queens. Well, you are actually. He didn't go all in so what can you do so you don't make it worth his while to stay in the hand?

You can try to raise him $10 and in this case he may call. If you go all in and he has enough money in his pocket to rebuy, he might call you to try and catch a miracle card.

With players like this who are action addicts, they will call you no matter what.

And if the turn comes like this (and it will once in awhile):

You will have to just force a smile, force the acid from coming up your throat and watch yourself lose no matter what. The comfort in this is that a player like your opponent will go bust and a lot of times in the same session after a few hours. They have a lot of lucky hours but they might end up with unlucky days when the dust settles.

I've talked to some players and for the most part, they still remember the few times that they win with cards that come at the last minute. I am tempted to ask some of them, and I do this of my friends, "But how many times have you tried that and lost?" Generally you get a "I dunno" and a shrug of the shoulders. It is random reinforcement. People tend to remember the things they want rather than what actually has happened.

Hey, the truth can hurt but it is better in business and in gambling that you at least be honest with yourself so you don't end up bluffing yourself out of your money in the long run.

Kim Greenblatt on being profitable if you have special needs people who need caring

Sunday, August 03, 2008, 10:00:37 PM | admin

Let's face it, you aren't going to live forever. Try as you might sooner or later (hopefully later) you will be out of this sphere of existence. It is hard enough planning for your family and their needs as is but it is harder if you are caring for a special needs relative.

It is important that you have whatever insurance you can in place and current. It is important that you have a guardian already in place to take care of your parent, child, grandchild, etc. in the event something happens to you. You don't want a judge to make an arbitrary decision as to who should be taking care of your special needs loved one.

Are you saving enough now? I know, I know - money is tight, you may lose your job (maybe you aren't working) but it is important to try and have enough cash stashed away.

What about special long term considerations if something happens to you that prevents you from taking care of that person? Costs for long term care rocket if you don't plan for them early on and get insurance where you can for yourself. The Federal Government allows great tax breaks if you are currently paying for Long Term Care insurance.

2008
For 2008, the maximum amount of qualified long-term care premiums you can include as medical expenses has increased. You can include qualified long-term care premiums, up to the amounts shown below, as medical expenses on Schedule A (Form 1040)

- Age 40 or under – $310.
- Age 41 to 50 – $580.
- Age 51 to 60 – $1,150.
- Age 61 to 70 – $3,080.
- Age 71 or over – $3,850.

Note. The limit is for each person.

Those amounts above are for premium payments and surprisingly, the deductions for the medical expenses are pretty close to what the premium payments are for the long term coverage.

Please make sure you talk to other special needs parents about setting up a trust fund. You need something pretty bulletproof so any money that goes to your loved one is not going to be taxed or they might end up losing whatever other government benefits (like Medi-Cal, disability) that they are currently getting.

Please write your Congressmen (and women) as well as the Governors, and Presidential candidates. We are in a rough situation right now where if you make any kind of money, any kind of funding that helps a lot of special needs people will be yanked. Make your voices heard so that the people who can't talk for themselves to get the special care and assistance that they need, get heard. It is cliché to say that but it still is an effective cliché.

Make sure that you also trust the people that are taking care of your elderly or special needs charges on a daily basis. A lot of people are in the health care field for the money and not for the calling to help others. That is fine by me and they are entitled to make a profit as long as they do their job and do it well. After all they are taking care of our daughters, sons, parents, grandparents, relatives and ultimately in some cases, us.

Please drop me a post as to what you might want to see tax wise or business wise in terms of special needs. I have a daughter who has Rett Syndrome and I get where you are coming from. You don't want to gamble if you can help it with something like this.

A portion of all my book sales from all my books goes to finding a cure for Rett Syndrome and research to make girls suffering with Rett Syndrome lives a little easier. Rett Syndrome affects a girl born every fifteen minutes. Most boys born with the Rett gene die at birth. Rett is not Tourette. That is a different syndrome.

Kim Greenblatt

Improve Your Product or Service With Each Release By Kim Greenblatt

Monday, August 04, 2008, 10:10:00 PM | admin

Unless you have a perfect product out of the chute every time, and if you do, please call me or drop me an email because I want to work for you, you constantly should be looking at what you can do to improve your product, your service, your research.

An example of this is my first book, Your Daughter Has Been Diagnosed With Rett Syndrome. It was my first self published book and it wasn't heavy in the number of pages, and in fact, I added a flip book inside which chewed up pages but still it was fairly well received. The reason is that people searching for information are pretty forgiving if they get the information they are looking for. In the case of my first book, I have been lucky and one of these days I need to get a sequel out with changes in Arianna that have been happening and our lives in general (from the perspective of coping parents).

My poker books were presented differently and there have been various comments on them ranging from hatred to delight. I think the truth is somewhere in between that I didn't right the great American poker book but something that had some practical value to the reader (hence the name of my series of books that start off "Practical").

I did get better with subsequent books though my experiment into larger print for the Crazy Pineapple 8b book was either appreciated by the older set or booed and hissed. Sales have picked up on the book and from emails I have been getting, I think again, that content is king and that is what people look for.

Incrementally, I decided to move onto cover illustrations and I added that for my fiction books, The Inappropriate Library and Clean, A Tale From The Inappropriate Library.

With each book - fiction or non-fiction, I get a little better and as the saying goes, instead of making a million mistakes I only make 999,999. The take away for you, dear reader, is try and list one or several things that you are doing that the next time you try to do it, you will have improved it someway.

The Japanese built up their economy from the 1960s thru 80s by incrementally just developing existing products. They did this by taking products like televisions and making them better, one thing at a time. They improved size, color picture, etc. They ended up owning large chunks of property for a brief time in the United States and companies like Sony are what people think of when it comes to electronics. Their overnight success was accomplished by gradually changing one thing at a time and releasing it.

Apple took a pocket mp3 player, repackaged it and marketed it as the must-have device and the iPod has taken off and is still flying several years later.

If you aren't making a product, think of what you can do with your service that will add value for your customer or client. The little things go a long way like being polite, taking the time to listen to the customer and getting the orders right the first time.

Hopefully I got the order right this time. Did you want some fries with that?

Kim Greenblatt

Taxes and UFOS-Unidentified Financial Obstacles

Tuesday, August 05, 2008, 10:10:28 PM | admin

Every tax season I run into people who have been abducted. That's right. They have been kidnapped by unidentified financial obstacles- that is a term that I coined that is very top secret. These ufos come along and teleport the money right out of their pockets and when it comes to tax time they sometimes are in a position where they don't have the money to pay their taxes.

Warnings that you may be a victim of ufo incident?

1. You have cashed out a 401K or retirement account early and haven't put aside at least a third of it for taxes for the Federal government or the state.
2. You have received a cash prize, gambling winnings and you have spent it all without putting money aside for taxes.
3. You have received a bonus from work and the taxes don't seem to be taken out however you already know that it will show up on a W-2 as income at the end of the year.
4. You have sold a screenplay and made a lot of money. If so, congratulations!

Folks, do yourselves a favor and force yourself to put aside at least a third of that money for paying taxes. Lock it in an interest bearing account or worse case, a checking account, and please try not to touch it. If you can, pay the money at the nearest financial quarter that you can or wait and make sure that at the end of the year that you have the money to pay for any taxes that are due.

Aliens laser beaming cities are almost welcome if when it comes tax time you find yourself owing thousands of dollars.

Whether you are planning on starting a business or dealing with day to day tax planning, please take the time to account for paying your taxes. I understand it isn't a popular position to take, but it is a dirty job and somebody has to do it!

While I am speaking about ufos, since they are unidentified financial obstacles, please try and get a savings program in place and definitely an emergency fund so when they ufos attack, you can fight back with cash.

If you are dealing with a person with special needs, I don't have to tell you about the money that gets disintegrated frequently when trying to make ends meet. That is all the more reason that you should try to be sensitive to any financial gifts that happen to come your way.

Be profitable (and happy and healthy)!

Get Attention, Keep It and Getting People To Buy Something

Wednesday, August 06, 2008, 10:11:02 PM | admin

It is next to impossible to monetize something on the Internet. You can try to stir up controversy and sometimes you can try the direct marketing approach. Unfortunately the approach below only works if you have shaved your head bald and your customers are all named Joey. Fortunately, my hair has grown back somewhat and there are other, better ways to do marketing.

First, don't try to be something you aren't. I wish I could write romantic fiction because if you are good at that you can make a lot of money. I don't have the chops for it. You'll note that none of my books are romantic fiction though I have dabbled with children's fiction and young adult horror. The reason I have written fiction books is because I think (and I have been told) that I am pretty good at it. Well, I've actually been told that my first book was kind of quick and the second one is better, but they both are part of an overall series. But I digress....

 Second, There is money to be made if your niche is big enough. Everybody is good at something. The question is can you monetize what you are good at. If you are good at more than one thing, like I am (ahem, hey it is my blog and I can leave modesty at the door), try and pick the one or two things to focus in on so you don't waste your energy.

Third, expect to be an overnight success after several years of work. It is rare that you will get the instant monetary recognition or even fame that you want right out of the chute. Remember, people may be tickled by a novelty but will they stick around and buy anything from you? Only if you can show them that you have something to say that hasn't been said before or you are showing them how to make some money.

Fourth, watch your costs in terms of money and time. Sure it is fun to be able to take an ad out in the American Super Bowl if you have a few million dollars. Will that really translate to sales though? The flip side is all that time you are using to make domino art, as cool as it looks, will it help you get gigs setting up falling domino exhibitions around the world? You can be the judge of that stuff yourself.

Fifth, whatever you do, be prepared in your business to be able to work the market so you don't end up having to close up shop so early. And be sure that you don't end up having so small a niche that you will be limiting yourself in your market.

Unless your market is everybody who has a name of Joey. (This was followed on the website with a link to a video of me calling out "Joey" a number of times. My cousin's name is Joey.)

Discipline and Attitude are "The Secret" keys to success in business and life

Thursday, August 07, 2008, 10:11:33 PM | admin

Almost sound liking a drill instructor, huh? I was talking with people on the Rettnet, one of the special needs support groups for people who have children who have Rett Syndrome and one of the things that came up was the discussion of the "The Secret". Basically, it is the Law of Attraction (what you can imagine you will get, Like Attracts Like, etc). I don't have too many gripes with it except for the fact that the so-called secret has been around forever in mystical teachings. It hasn't been taught to the masses because generally they need to have their bodies and minds tuned so that they can clearly broadcast what they really want and is it a noble, life and society affirming wish. Or at least that is how it is presented.

It seems today that everybody wants everything now and fast. I've talked about this before in some of my other posts. My cure for this in business, in relationships and in life is to tell people to be disciplined and be positive.

By being disciplined, that means that you don't give in to every impulse to by the latest gadget or goodie that is thrown in front of your face on television, the internet or anywhere.

That means that you need to get your family on board with discipline as well since it won't do you any good saving money or energy if everybody else leaves the lights on in every room when they aren't in it or spend their paychecks as fast as they get it - and then try to max out their credit cards. Sheesh!

I will not be going into some of the fundamental problems I have with the presentation of plans like the Secret, but I will say that positive thinking does work and overall I think that will power and desire are what drive the universe.

The problem I have is that everybody has all sorts of will power and desires that don't always go along with the wills or desires of everybody else. A lot of the time their desires don't even go along with the best interests of society as a whole and I thing it is best to leave the subject there for now!

I guess that is where things like social communities like blogs come in. For further discourses please post me a message. In the meantime, I need to practice what I am preaching and get back to working on my next book.

Kim Greenblatt

How Long Will the Bad Times Last?

Friday, August 08, 2008, 10:03:35 PM | admin

With the start of the Olympics, the celebration going on in China, I see a lot of good times happening. Unfortunately, here in Southern California, as well as other parts of the United States, I have to ask myself, as I am sure you do, dear reader, when will the bad times end?

People are getting laid off, people are losing their homes, and despite the drop in gasoline, people cannot afford to pay for gasoline, food and clothing.

These are basic items - food, clothing and shelter- that we have taken for granted in this country as inalienable rights. It is amusing because as we move into more of global capitalistic economy the only right that seems to matter is financial survival of the fittest.

It doesn't have to be this way and hopefully we are nearing the end of the bad times. A lot of people seem to put stock in whoever wins the presidential election. Maybe they are right because it looks like Congress is going to hold off on any major legislation until after January 2009. It will be interesting to follow up on this post to see what happens maybe a year from now. Let us hope that it isn't "business as usual".

I know in my own life I see people finding it harder and harder to make ends meet. Part of it may be their own doing for over-extending their credit. Hopefully this site will help them get back on track to being profitable or give them some ideas to get their lives turned around.

People trying to take care of special needs children, parents or relatives are being crushed by medical bills, higher drug costs and lack of support from their communities.

My suggestion, dear readers, is to start writing and if you can, screaming at our leaders. Our congressional representatives, senators, Governors and presidential candidates need to hear that we have to change things. We need to spend some money on rebuilding our infrastructure. Our bridges, highways, subways, and cities need to be rebuilt. If we get enough government bonds going we can not only get the money to get working, that will employee people. Employed people will spend their money while they are working. It will keep the circle called our economy going.

It won't happen overnight or be easy but it can happen. If you are reading this from outside the United States, welcome to the site and any suggestions or thoughts would be welcome as well.

Let the good times roll and let them please start rolling soon!!!!

Kim Greenblatt

Comic book rush is on and I give it two years

Saturday, August 09, 2008, 10:12:32 PM | admin

With the success of Iron Man, Wanted and the Dark Knight movies it looks like the next two to three years will be comic book movie years. It had been hit or miss with Marvel with hits like Spider-Man and some misses like the second Fantastic Four (movie). Warner Brothers DC Superman

Returns did okay but not as phenomenal as the Dark Knight movie.

How do you profit from this?

If you are a creator or owner of comic book character rights, this is the time to pitch your characters since studios are gobbling up comic book stories or trying to build their franchise. Disney will be developing in house their own comic book line characters apart from what they license already. I give the window two to three years before people get tired of them since these things seem to go in cycles. I may be completely wrong here but that is my story and I am sticking with it.

If you own comic book related collectibles, now is the time to sell your Watchmen comics with the movie coming out, anything related to recent comic book movies or collectibles. It has been my experience that after the movie is out is a bad time unless you are one of the first people who can buy or sell the collectible item.

My motto on collectibles is that if you sold it a profit, count your blessings. You don't want to be the owner of a mint condition set of Watchmen comics at $400 if you cannot sell them for $150 two years later!

If you are planning on buying anything for speculation I would stick with rare items. Limited items from the Comic Con, true items of scarcity are the way to go. That is the way to get collectors interested in buying something from you and better yet, to pay top dollar.

I posted on somebody else's blog a comment about what happens if a movie that costs $180 million dollars fails at the box office? A lot of studio people will cry and even worse, they will stop making movies in that genre for awhile because they goofed with the previous film.

Follow the entertainment companies like Marvel, Disney and Warner Brothers. Keep in mind that if they have other divisions other than their movie division they may net out with a loss despite a great year in their film division. Also, film division profits are notoriously all over the map.

Due your own due diligence, super friends!

Special Needs Sensitivity and Business

Sunday, August 10, 2008, 10:10:47 PM | admin

I've noticed at amusement parks and some places that for special needs people, there are certain hoops that a person has to jump through now to get passes for special access. Some parks have modified their rides to be wheelchair friendly to the point where you can literally take your wheelchair on a rollercoaster.

Some parks though have gotten pretty tight with granting access because so many jerks and lazy slobs have abused the special needs pass access. Because somebody is tired they should NOT be given a wheelchair. Sit down and rest. If they actually have a documented condition, that is fine with me. Bring a doctor's note with you otherwise you are taking access away from my daughter and others like her.

I am tired of the Carlos Mencia (that isn't even his real first name, by the way, he uses it to sound more Latino) nonsense about people expecting special needs people to say that others are either better than that. His harping on special needs because they are an easy target is nonsense. If he ever has a child or relative born with special needs he will sing a different tune.

To be fair, there are some special needs comics who use their disabilities as part of their routine. More power to them I say. For a lot of people who can't speak to defend themselves, all they are asking for is a little bit of courtesy.

At one of the amusement parks in Southern California, we had people give us grief about Arianna trying to get a pass. One look at my daughter and as gorgeous as she is you can see that she, due to her hang-wringing from Rett Syndrome has something going on. The guy gave us the party line until we basically showed him the pass we had last time. Sharren and I had gone to the park with our documentation in the past.

Also, please tell all everybody that special needs chairs and access are there for special needs people first people. Get your freaking baby strollers out of the way. We had an instance where we were cut off by a family with a stroller. Not cool. The amusement park employees were on it and corrected the situation. Kudos all around!

Our money is just as good as people's money who don't have special needs relatives. I can just as easily find another venue where my wife, kids and relatives can go to spend more money.

Have any rants or bones to rattle about special needs and business? How about people who aren't disabled using driving cards they shouldn't? Let me know your beefs here.

Part of all my book proceeds go to research finding a cure for Rett Syndrome and reversal of symptoms.

Tropic Thunder Timothy Shriver, Chairman of Special Olympics and boycotts

Monday, August 11, 2008, 10:03:45 PM | admin

In the Rett Syndrome community as well as in other special needs communities, there is some buzz about Timothy Shriver's op ed piece in the Washington Post. Evidently in the upcoming film, Tropic Thunder, there will be exchanges where the actors talk about playing characters who have special needs and are called "retarded".

Not having seen the movie nor read the script, I cannot say myself what is being said but I can say one thing. It looks like there may be some decision to boycott the film by the National Down Syndrome Congress and the national ARC (if I have my information correct). All politically correct heated debate put aside, how does this relate to business and being profitable?

Well, if enough groups get together to boycott a film, it won't be seen. It depends on the spending money of the groups as well as the total bad publicity - or perception of bad publicity that will be out there. Remember the OJ book where he told how he might have killed his late wife?

In the previews, it shows Morton Downey Jr having undergone surgery to transform from a white man into a black man for acting. Okay, was that a concession to also show how edgy and funny they are? I dunno yet. If this is part of the satire, I get it. That will help in the movie's overall box office.

Readers of my blog know that I have an open mind and a sense of humor so I am going to refrain from saying anything until I see the movie myself. I am not a hypocrite. If it is funny, it is funny.

The problem is, I agree with Timothy Shriver that the movie is going after a group of people who can't defend themselves. I've had the same issue with Carlos Mencia. Surprisingly, or maybe not so, I haven't had this problem with South Park because they are truly equal opportunity offenders.

I also don't know what kind of agenda Mr. Shriver has and maybe he is mad because he didn't get a shot at reviewing the movie. Again, I don't know and it is beyond my paygrade, folks.

So, back to the business angle...

How much economic pull will this have on the movie if there is a boycott? It is hard to tell because it may backfire and make the movie a big hit because it has been boycotted by all sorts of special needs groups. People may go see it to see what the fuss was all about. Remember, controversy gets people interested in seeing something.

If enough people don't see it though or it dries up quickly, it maybe because it was a horrible movie, period. Maybe the satire is above people's heads. I dunno. Lately, when a lot of comedies are just over-packing their movie with lowest common denominator jokes hoping some will stick they are finding that people can get that stuff for free over the internet and they run away. If the movie can generate $10 worth of laughs per person multiplied by 100 million people, with or without the special needs jokes it will be a hit, even if there is a boycott.

Stuff like this happens all the time. It use to be to become a hit in the United Kingdom you use to say something bad about the royal family to get banned from the radio and you would be a hit.

An interesting fact is that I was probably going to see the movie without all the attention being called to it. In the previews it looks like they are three clueless actors. In the roles they are playing you are expecting to hear nonsense come out of their mouths. My hope is that they don't dwell on the special needs humor as one aspect of it.

Should we just ignore the protests and see what happens with this movie? You need to come to the decision yourself. As for me, I will see the movie for myself and make my own decisions afterwards.

How are your tax preparation plans coming?

Tuesday, August 12, 2008, 10:05:48 PM | admin

Pretty funny to hear that in August isn't it? Not really. Maybe you need to scrounge around for those receipts for your donations. Maybe times were tough and you had to cash out your 401k or IRA. Regardless of what is going on in your life, you should always have a pulse on your money and your taxes - no matter what country you are living in.

For those of my readers here in the United States, quarterly taxes are due in usually on 4/15 for the first quarterly payment, 6/15 for the second payment, 9/15 for the third payment and 1/15 of the next year for the fourth payment. You can save yourself a lot of grief and financial hardship by paying any taxes that you owe if you won a lottery, received a bonus or had a great quarter and you are self employed. Remember that the United States tax system is a pay as you go system and that you are responsible for payments and penalties if they are late or there is an underpayment.

If you live in a state where you have an obligation for state taxes, perhaps you may want to check out this page (my site has the current state department of taxation or revenue information).

If you are running a business, make sure that you have all your receipts if you are doing your own taxes or put them aside for your tax preparer. If you can, update your books with purchases, sales and keep them current. It will make things easier at tax time when you prepare your statements of income, balance sheet and any supporting paperwork.

If you have any other licensing requirements for your business, make sure they are current. The chances are that they are also a tax deduction so save the receipts showing that you made the payments.

If you are planning any major lifestyle changes (like adopting a child or getting married), be sure to save receipts for anything to do with the adoption. If you are planning on getting married, congratulations and may I strongly suggest you read this page (it is the one on Bad Tax Idea, Good Tax Idea-Not Talking Money before getting Married) in my site? Not planning your taxes nor talking over your income and spending habits is not the best way to start off a honeymoon and yet it is one of the most common issues I find with people when I help them with their tax preparation.

Maybe you are uncomfortable with my advice? You can find other information but remember that when it comes to tax preparation you can ask ten different tax pros and get ten different answers. Fortunately, if you ask me a question I try to give you just one answer - the right one!

Don't be afraid of asking questions now. If you wait until later in the year it may be too late to undo any damage that is done. Your best bet is to contact tax professionals or start doing your own research now. It will save you a lot of aggravation after December 31, when for a lot of things, it is too late to adjust the situation for taxes.

Kim Greenblatt Asks If You Teach Your Children About Money While They Are Young

Wednesday, August 13, 2008, 10:01:57 PM | admin

Where do kids learn their first values about money? From mom and dad. Or from your baby's mom, or your baby's dad. Whoever. The people that will introduce a strong sense of monetary education into your kids at first will be you. What kind of example are you being for them?

Are you a saver? Have you shown them that they need to start saving money, even if it is with a piggy bank and just small change once a week?

Are you a spender? Do you buy everything you want, when you want it regardless of the cost? Do you end up charging up your credit cards in order to do that? Not a good idea. Do you want to have another generation of kids piling up debt?

I love America. I love the fact that capitalism is all over the globe. What I don't love is the mass marketing and media shoving ads from the internet, from tv shows, from the radio from magazines trying to tell my kids what they "need" to have. They can get by on a lot less than they think they can and yes, like any devoted parent I want what is best for them but I would be doing my son a disservice by giving him everything he wants. In Arianna's case, <u>Arianna has Rett Syndrome</u>, I am doing all that I can to make her life comfortable and help her develop her communication skills.

There is a difference between teaching children to be frugal and cheap. Frugal is where you save a little bit of money from each weekly allowance, paper route, usher job at the theater, etc. You put that into a savings account for something big later on. You get your children use to saving for emergencies and a rainy day. Cheap is not leaving a tip to a waiter or waitress at a restaurant who gave you great service. If they give you lousy service, you can teach your children at that point the value of good service by still leaving a tip, just a small one. They may not say anything but they will get the message.

Teach them about money to avoid <u>gambling schemes</u> as well.

Special needs kids can get the message too. They need to learn - and some learn it quite well and quickly - the need to price shop, to learn the difference in value with some items and to see through marketing at times.

If you are reading my blogs, I am sure you are teaching your kids the value of money. While you are at it, you may want to look into getting them a Roth IRA if they are working a part time job as well.
It doesn't hurt to start their retirement while they are young.

If they have questions about money, please encourage them. Any ideas about making money also should be encouraged. If they want to start a part time business, do what you can to help them. You never know. They may become the next garage start-up billionaire.

Do We Need Therapy When We Do Our Taxes or Just Forgiveness?

Thursday, August 14, 2008, 10:05:08 PM | admin

When I prepared taxes for one lady several years ago, she was in need of getting relief from having some credit card debt removed. She received from the credit card companies some 1099-Cs. She was worried because the forgiven debt was going to look like income.

"What should I do?" she asked.

"Taxpayers may qualify for one of several exclusions that allow them to reduce taxable income from canceled debts." I said. " If the exclusions apply, they must file an IRS form 982 in addition to the 1099-C. The exclusions include debts discharged during bankruptcy and debts of consumers who are insolvent (meaning their liabilities exceed their assets) prior to the cancellation of the debt. However, the exclusion applies only up to the amount by which consumers are insolvent."

"What does that mean?"

"It means in your case that you don't have to worry because you had $3,000 in debts that were forgiven and liabilities exceeded assets by $1,800, then the $1,800 would be excluded as income. "The remaining $1,200 would be reported under other income."

When everything settled for that particular year after reviewing everything she presented to me, she ended up getting a refund.

"I'm seeing a therapist, Kim." she said looking at me really really intently. "Do you think I should continue it?"

"If you feel you are getting value from it, sure."

When she left that year she said, "I am going to keep my eye on you, Kim."

Yikes. Tax preparer stalkers! "Thanks!"

She came back in better financial shape having listened to me over the next few years and is in a happy relationship.

The moral of this story? There is no moral, just keep me away from people who get extra creepy and say they want to keep an eye on me. Well, that, and it pays to be current in your tax knowledge.

Getting forgiveness for credit card debt is great but remember that it will be reported as income from the credit card company so you should review with a tax professional what exactly your tax liability (if any) might be at tax time. Try to do it early so you can have money to pay for the taxes if you owe or so you can gleefully anticipate a refund.

And make sure that you don't tell your tax pro that you are going to stalk him or her!

Was Your Trip To The Olympic Games Tax Deductible?

Friday, August 15, 2008, 10:08:09 PM | admin

I received one email asking if a person went to China to see the Summer Games if their trip would be considered a tax deduction. No, it would not. The basic rule of thumb for business is that the travel has to be related to business. It has to be documented. The time, date and duration of the trip as well as the intent, are all required pieces of information that should be tracked. If you can, make notes as to the result of the meeting or business seminar. If the meeting resulted in you getting the sale, great.

In case you are audited by the IRS or your respective state tax agency, you will need to be able to substantiate the deductions that you are claiming.

Now, if as part of the trip you decided to go see a swimming event and were fortunate enough to get tickets, you could see the event but not write anything off. If the nature of your trip was predominantly to go to have a business meeting, no problem. The Olympics were a one day side trip.

If, however, you are one of the millions of people who have gone to China I hope that you are giving the IRS and the state agencies some credit. Do you think that they aren't aware that the Olympics are going on?

What do you think the chances are that they will go ahead and really burrow to see if you actually had a business trip or were just trying to run a fast one on them if you are claiming a trip to China from July thru August? If you thought that your chances were pretty good, you win the gold medal for avoiding audits. Please let common sense prevail. It will save you hassles in the long run.

For more information check out the Internal Revenue Service website and search on business deductions. You might find Publication 463, Travel, Entertainment, Gift and Car Expenses, to be of some interest. I also touch on some good ideas in my tax book, "Bad Tax Idea, Good Tax Idea". Tax laws change so it pays to stay current on what can be deducted for your business expenses. Consult a tax professional if you don't like doing the research yourself.

If you are parents or a relative of an Olympic contender, congratulations to you and your relative! Think of the trip as an adventure, supporting your loved one and I hope you are having (or had) the time of your life! To all my domestic and international readers, please keep the spirit of competition on a friendly level and thanks for reading.

Star Wars victorious over Tropic Thunder?

Saturday, August 16, 2008, 10:07:24 PM | admin

As much as I wanted to go see Tropic Thunder, I was too tired from working the other day. It is on hold as much due to my exhaustion as to my son's desire to see the Star Wars movie instead. So, the upshot on this is pretty much the way I expected it to go. Normally I see every movie but in this case because of work obligations and time schedules, I have to pick and choose my movies. Because Tropic Thunder chose a mid week opening such as Wed to try and get more box office money (and I am guessing to get a jump on Clone Wars) they may have had their shot at the golden ticket and it may be over.

I still would like to see the movie but I am not going out of my way to and it may be that I might forget about it because of the dearth of other movies coming out that I want to see. That is a problem with the movie blockbuster model. You have to make your money fast before the next contender zooms up on you and tries to get all the buzz and movie ticket money.

From what I read, Tropic Thunder had a decent first night opening of six million dollars or something close to that. Whether it is good to enough of a start, I am going to hold off judgment since I think that the Star Wars fans are going to bury anything that hits the movies this weekend.

If you have a good brand like Star Wars, you create your own buzz with the fans and certainly with a thirty plus year pedigree of marketing and product, I think any movie, controversial or not will not fare well against the Clone Wars. So how was Clone Wars?

It was action packed, non-stop fun and adventure. I hope it does well in the box office!

May the Force and making money be with you!

He Who Pays The Piper Calls The Tune

Sunday, August 17, 2008, 10:08:24 PM | admin

I received an interesting e-mail asking me about changing products to suit customer's needs. I am all for it. The old cliché, "He Who Pays The Piper Calls The Tune", should be the watchword of the future but sadly, some people just don't get to pick the music they want to. Consider that if you buy a computer, the operating system that ships with it may have bugs. It is not a final product. That may not mean it is a bad product - far from it, but it is the voices of the people who pay for the machines and software that complain and they should get what they want.

Voting with your pocketbook is one of the greatest strengths in the international capitalistic market that we are in. Oil prices have dropped because people have dialed back on their driving in the United States and decided to save their money. When the want to spend money, they want to try and do it on their own terms. When it came to gasoline, however, it had to hit a market hurt point where people could just not afford to pay the high prices. Well, extra oil has been pumped and there is at least (for now) a little more out there. Basic economics of supply and demand kick in here.

But what about if you are entertainment for somebody's wedding? What if the groom, who is writing the check for your band, asks to sit in on the drums? What do you do? If you are a shrewd business person as well as musician, you ask the drummer to sit out a set and let the groom sit in.

Putting ego aside you will be part of a lot of pictures and possibly the band to be called for all the social functions for this family. One would think this is common sense in business but so many individuals and companies like to force upon their customers what they want them to have. In some businesses, it may make no difference but if it is something that you or I can modify, sure, let me try and change it up.

The companies that offer the most versatility will make more money in the long run because people will pay for what they want. People will find money to spend for things they want. Isn't it a great idea then to give the customer exactly what they want if you can? Remember, if you don't, there is another website, blog or store down the block waiting to fill in the niche for you!

Project Management and Cost Cutting

Monday, August 18, 2008, 10:11:11 PM | admin

For a lot of companies, there have been money management issues of Olympic proportions. One of the best things that a project manager can do in terms of cost cutting is to review his or her project and take stock of any things that can be trimmed from the project in terms of cost.

Generally two things happen if there is a downcycle in a company with a project:

1. The scope of the project gets reduced.

2. The project gets cancelled completely.

If this is your only project and it looks like you won't be reassigned to any new projects what can you do?

If the company wants to keep the project going, you will need to be able start finding major places to cut costs. Plan on working at a lower level of spending than you were before. It may not save the project but it may keep it going for awhile longer in the hopes that the economy will change, that there may be a cash infusion or something will happen to change circumstances.

If the project is going to get cancelled, there isn't much you can do about it except let your staff know as soon as management lets you know (and they give you permission to tell them). Most employees keep their ear to the ground at a company and in these trying times can tell if there are money problems.

Try to make sure that your resume is current and the best of luck to you. If you have been through these business cycles before, you can see that they follow the expansion and contractions of business spending in a country. Ultimately, if people are living somewhere, things will get developed again. Whether the project is for building a factory or writing the new web portal, eventually the work that will not get done now may end up getting done somewhere and sometime else.

It is up to you to make sure you are around it be able to do it though if you want to. If the work doesn't come back, like the Olympics, if you have trained and have discipline, there is a chance for medal somewhere else later on.

Make Sure That Your Business Plans All Come Together

Tuesday, August 19, 2008, 10:03:24 PM | admin

If you have taken the time to write your business plan, prepare for your business, consider what type of business you want, you have figured out what tax issues you have for the state you live in, and now what?

Well, if things are going well, you should have your contingency plan in place and you shouldn't be taking any gambles that you don't have to. So, you start looking at what is going on day to day and what you can do to improve it. Make sure that your credit is in good shape because if you plan on growing at any time in the future, you may need to borrow money.

If you have enough money of your own, great. Most people though, even with money, find that their businesses need more than they generally have.

Don't be locked in your plans. The marketplace changes now faster than ever. If you need to, plan with your staff, partners or stockholders for changes to stay profitable. If you find that you are losing money, it is time to step back and see if there is something that you change in your business.

Make sure that your insurance and bonds are current if you have them or need them.

Ask your customers how you are doing. They won't be bashful. If you are doing a great job, get their testimonials. If not, see what you can do to improve your business and you will watch everything come together!

If you employ staff, ask them for feedback and try not to take it personally otherwise they will lie to you. If you have a bad rapport with your staff, think about changing it. If there are people who are working for you who really aren't working for you - meaning that they are lazy, not taking their work seriously, you need to think about replacing them. There are plenty of people looking for work right now and there are a lot of good workers out there.

So keep your plans in order, make sure you are acting on them and review them. Your plans for your business will help materialize what your business has planned for you!

Self Publishing and Self Realization and The Depression Word

Wednesday, August 20, 2008, 10:04:04 PM | admin

I have just finished the edit for my next book, **Practical Money Making-Surviving Recession, Layoffs, Credit Problems, Generating Passive Income Streams, Working Full Time or Part Time and Retirement**. As I start the post production process and the cover generation I realized that I used the "D" word in the book.

That's right, I said it. Depression.

Back in our great-grandfathers or for some of us, grandfathers day, in the 1920s, there was what they called the Great Depression. The problem back then was that banks had over-extended themselves because of bad investments in the stock market and speculation. In this day and age, we are hearing daily of more and more financial problems due to the housing bubble popping.

This is the time to start looking to how to make money during a depression. It may not be another Great Depression but with inflation rising, interest rates flat, Home Equity loans frozen and the next shoe to drop will be credit card companies freezing lines, it is time to get income and expectations in line for the immediate future.

What will sell? Well, I suspect my book will have brisk sales if I keep the price at the market friendly $15-20 range (it will probably go for $15 retail before online bookstore discounting) and people continue to look for extra ways to make money, invest their money and work to get out of debt. The price point for non-fiction is generally between $12-25 depending on the book and content.

Did I have some other self-realizations? Of course! Let me share my realizations with you, dear reader.

Look for businesses you can start or continue that will help people save money, something that they can do that will save their homes, put food on their plates. This is going to be a rough ride for all of us and if the economic forecasts look true, it may be two to four years for the U.S. to get out of the slump.

In terms of investments, I would watch very carefully what I would be putting my money into because for at least the next few months, there is going to be turmoil with looming military conflicts on the Russian border, uncertainty over the Presidential elections and the bottom of the financial markets meltdown may not be over yet. I invite you to do your own financial research and come to your own conclusions.

Here is an important reminder to people starting a business in the coming months or years. People will still pay for something that they think they will need, so marketing will still have some affect. The reality is that they will not be able to go into debt anymore to buy the item they want so they will have to wait patiently and longingly like a kid looking at a new video game in a store window.

From what I understand, in some of the hotels in Macau, the island off of China, the big casinos do get a lot of people but a lot of them just come over with their bagged lunch and sit and look at the slot machines and gaming tables. That is shockingly similar to state line casinos here in the United States between California and Nevada. It means that just because there is something marketed attractively to a customer - and there is nothing that screams marketing like a slot machine - that doesn't mean that they will have the money to use it.

Maybe they need to have lower cost slot machines or table limits at some of the casinos in Macau to accommodate their poorer players. Maybe the casino builders and owners are discovering that even high rollers and whales go through their own financial depression and not have enough money to go play at the casinos. Time will tell and for now, that is outside of my pay grade, folks.

The take away from this is that personal depression may result from financial depression but if you are aware of what is happening you can plan accordingly for it by adjusting your income expectations and turn your depression into a great self-realization impression!

Good luck to you and may you be profitable, happy, healthy and safe in all your ventures.

Cleaning and Your Business

Thursday, August 21, 2008, 11:18:00 PM | admin

Tonight I spent the night going through my office and throwing away papers that have literally been sitting on my desk for years. We are talking some Target store receipts dating back to 1991. I don't even think I have the shirts that were on that receipt. I am sure I probably wouldn't fit into the shirt as well.

What does this have to do with you? It means that you should at least once a year take stock of your business or job and see where you can clean things up. Maybe you are a little slow with dealing with problems. Maybe you react too quickly and that causes more problems some times.

These are the things that you can tweak as you become aware of them. In some businesses, you can't win no matter what. If you are a tax collector people will not be happy with you no matter what you do.

Some other things to tweak are asking yourself where else can you improve productivity? Maybe there is something literally that you need to clean up. If you are in the restaurant business and find that you didn't get that "A" rating if you are in Los Angeles, California, you are probably wondering what else you can do to boost your health rating for your food.

Maybe you have some money leaks in your business and it is time to start plugging them up. It isn't the big losses that sometimes kill us, it can be the small nickel and dime losses or differences that will add up and cumulatively be a problem.

So make sure that when you clean your house, you also remember to do some cleaning at your business. Now I need to take a shower because all this sitting in dust and dirt is starting to make me itch....

More On Business Summer Fall Cleaning

Saturday, August 23, 2008, 6:57:05 AM | admin

Our Spring cleaning has drifted more into Fall cleaning with Labor Day coming up soon. As I started to say in the previous article, there is no time like the present to retool and streamline one's business plan.

Project Managers, CEOS and sole proprietors are all trying to cut costs and increase profit. In sales we are seeing more and more of smaller bags of items like potato chips, candy bars and the like. The prices either stay the same or go up slightly. While I applaud the fact that I can keep my weight down (and I am limiting the amount of junk food I am eating on general health principles-moderation is great for everybody) there are a lot of other people who will feel ripped off.

In the fast food business, some companies, like Carl's Jr, have taken the opposite approach and are big on loading you up with extra meat and larger hamburger buns. In other companies, like McDonald's, they are starting to see that they aren't making the kind of profit margin that they use to because of higher energy and food costs on their dollar menu items. They are kind of stuck though because a lot of Moms hit the drive thru and spend $25 on 25 dollar items for their families instead of ordering the higher priced value meals. McDonald's isn't quite sure at this point how they want to raise their prices because that might result in less people going to their restaurant.

It is important to realize that in the United States and other parts of the world right now, there is a financial contraction happening. The best advice that I can give somebody right now is to try something on a small scale and if it works, duplicate it at a larger scale.

I might limit some of the dollar items or start with one of them at the fast food restaurant and see how sales go. This isn't a novel idea and it has happened before when Coca Cola tried to move over to the "New Coke" formula. People hated it.

People hate change even more when it costs more money. They tend to adjust accordingly though. When gas prices passed over $4 a gallon in Southern California, people started driving less. It was economics in action that the market sweet spot to get people to stop spending money on gas was upwards of $4. Now that prices have dropped somewhat, there is slightly more driving.

The same correlation can hold true in business where you can see if your sales are not going to be affected dramatically by cutting out some loss leaders, give them a shot.

The net result of summer or fall business cleaning is a nice, clean profitable income statement!

Kim Greenblatt

Job Searching - How You Can Tell Things Are Slow

Saturday, August 23, 2008, 10:17:18 PM | admin

One of the ways that you can tell that things are slow in an economy and hiring is tough is if the company website is in "desperate need" to fill a position "ASAP" and they refer you to an automated system to just through your resume into their database.

Another ways is when recruiters try the bait and switch on you to get you to send them their resume. Depending on what part of the country you live in and where in the United States (or world for that matter), you may be seeing more of a "bust" economy rather than a "booming" one.

Companies are reacting accordingly and sending out postings hoping that things will get better. In some cases they are back to business as usual with their hopes that in this bad economy that they can get a Harvard PhD with 20 years experience in their field to work for minimum wage. Business has always been that way.

A subtler technique is where they post a position for say a technical engineer but when you get on board you find yourself doing Project Manager work. Or if you get hired on as a Project Manager and find yourself managing multiple projects and divisions doing a Director's job! It may not matter to you because you are just looking to get an income stream going again. If you are doing a great job, once economic times change, you are in a position for lobbying for more money.

Keep busy sending out resumes.

Start looking to see if there are any short term contracts that you can take, if that makes financial sense to you, to get some money coming in. If your industry is in a slump, like the auto industry, is there anything else where your skills can be used where you can derive a living?

I am getting a lot of emails from people talking about their frustrations at finding work. I tell that that eventually some of the ads they answer have to be legitimate ones and ultimately all it takes is one job. Once you get that one job, the rest of it will not matter.

Good luck!

Kim Greenblatt

Upcoming Book Chapter Listings - Practical Money Making

Sunday, August 24, 2008, 10:17:57 PM | admin

I just uploaded this weekend my book and cover to the printer. Hopefully I will have a clean proof and be out with the new book within a week. In the meantime, dear readers, here are the chapters for you to review and be amused with (or not depending on your mood).

Chapter Titles for the upcoming book, **Practical Money Making - Surviving Recession, Layoffs, Credit Problems, Generating Passive Income Streams, Working Full Time or Part Time and Retirement**.

If you, my readers, have any questions, please let me know. The book should be out in stores and available on the internet in about a month. The isbn number is 978-60622-001-6, and the suggested retail price in the United States will be $14.95.

Also, I am taking requests for what my next non-fiction book should be. Let me know what you want to see. In the front running is now a book on Special Needs. It will be more of a general book than my Rett Syndrome book and will focus on financial issues as well as social, physical, mental and spiritual things.

Let me know your thoughts. Be well, safe and profitable!

Kim Greenblatt

Market Price Point and Profitability

Monday, August 25, 2008, 10:07:22 PM | admin

One of the questions that I get asked is how do I determine price point for marketing a product. For something that there is already an established market for, say a book on a certain topic, the answer is straight forward. You price it with whatever else is selling close to that price in the market. You try to add value by presenting an engaging product or service that will be justified at whatever reasonable price that you put on it.

In the case of non-fiction books, the market sweet spot is around $12-20 for something that helps a person financially or personally. For specific niche books, such as gambling, one can go higher because the potential return is higher if the person who buys your book or product uses it and it works. The extra $2-5 in the long run will be recovered quickly. It makes economic and profitable sense to charge a little more. The online booksellers will also discount accordingly if the book takes off.

For new products that hit the market the answer is a little hazier. First, the initial development costs have to be recovered somehow. It could be that the cost of materials that you are using is pretty steep. A good example is the introduction of new video game console systems. Whenever a new system is introduced, until the new chips and guts of the system can be made relatively cheaply, the new system generally gets sold at a loss. Take a look at the Playstation and Xbox systems when they first came out. Over a few years, as Sony and Microsoft find more competitive (and quality) manufacturers, the can lower their price.

The market sweet spot for gaming systems use to be $300-350 but has dropped because of money being tight to $175-250.

The bigger companies can afford to take losses initially on their developmental bleeding edge systems because they have income streams from other products. In Microsoft's case they have their money coming in from the operating system sales and productivity tools. Sony has their media library and other entertainment hardware to sell.

You, as an individual or start-up person have to take into account the artificial or real need for your product in the price as well. If you are marketing a ray gun that makes people live forever, you can charge a very high price because a lot of people would pay anything for immortality. If you are trying to market a can opener that sings the theme song from the Olympics, you will have limited success and seasonal issues since something like that would only sell once every two years (for Winter or Summer Olympics). You can't also mark-up a can opener too much because people can get a similar silent product cheaper at their local dollar, thrifts or supermarkets.

Once a price point is established, you have to be flexible enough to lower it or raise it if your operating costs change or demand goes up. Look at oil. Gasoline prices rose or fell based on demand - real or perceived. The gas stations that kept their prices higher had less business.

Whether it is gas, can openers, immortality rays, video game consoles or books on Rett Syndrome, nobody gets something for free and it pays to price things appropriately.

Plugging Cash leaks

Tuesday, August 26, 2008, 10:07:57 PM | admin

A recent reader question to me was:

"Kim, how can I stop the money from being spent from my sole proprietorship? I am watching my money, tightened down on credit and am working on increasing sales."

The reader didn't tell me specifics and I can't say what is or what isn't being spent. I would think that he should be able to react faster than a corporation but I have no clue as to what this person's savings are.

So here are some general plugs to fit any size sink where money is being lost down the drain.

1. If you are a sole prop, watch your expenses. If business is down, see where you can cut expenses. You need to still advertise to keep a market presence but be ruthless in getting rid of advertising that isn't working.

2. Determine if you are married or have a significant other, that you or your partner aren't bleeding off excess cash that could be used to run the business. If that is the case, shame on you! Time to change and read some of my blogs on savings.

3. Examine shrinkage precautions. If you subcontract or hire part timers, look for shrinkage. That is the fancy word for theft. Are inventories dropping and the money isn't showing up to cover the missing product? Time to install cameras if you own a store.

Are you sure you can trust your business partner? I mean, really sure? A lot of times, spouses or lovers refuse to look at the obvious that their BFFD (best friend forever, dear or by five finger discount?) is cleaning them out.

Take appropriate steps and take action.

The only person who can insure that the leaks get plugged and the caulking stays in the bowl of your business if you are the one who does it. If you are paying for outside consultants or contractors, listen to what they say, even if you don't agree with them. If they are the experts in the field you are working in, they are the ones who might be able to help you turn the faucets on with more financial pressure and get you a gusher of cash!

Kim Greenblatt

Respect Confidentiality In Any Settlement

Wednesday, August 27, 2008, 10:17:40 PM | admin

This may be common knowledge for a lot of people but it bears repeating. If you get a court settlement and the terms are that it is confidential, please respect it. There is too much at risk to blab over it.

As a mediator and arbitrator for the Los Angeles and Santa Monica bar, I know firsthand that silence is more than golden when it comes to legal agreements. It is the law. It is required. That is why I couldn't believe that I was in an elevator the other day with two strange men and one of them was telling the other the details of some court settlement he was in. What if I was a from the courthouse and familiar with his case? What if I were a junior (well, okay senior) partner of the law firm that was against him and overheard him? I could march my overhearing butt back to court and get the judgment thrown out.

Folks, please respect the sanctity of the settlement. It doesn't matter if the settlement came from a trial, arbitration or a mediation. If you think of the aggravation you have gone through to get it, the pain, the madness, the anger, possibly the seemingly endless depositions, the soul-wrenching testimony in front of total strangers, it isn't worth it just for bragging rights.

This is especially important when it comes to dealing with special needs clients that you are responsible for. The person you are caring for may not understand what has happened and it would be horrible to get services removed, funds cancelled or worse because you had an attack of ego.

I am sure it won't happen if you remember this post. I suppose I shouldn't be so shocked at human nature. I think one of the first things that people like to do when they hear good ideas is tell it to the world. In this specific situation, it is better to keep it from the world! To do anything else just doesn't make sense and isn't profitable!

Kim Greenblatt

Good Planning for Finances Beats After The Fact Second Guessing

Thursday, August 28, 2008, 10:09:47 PM | admin

The problem with financial planning is that it is boring. Everybody wants to hear the latest and greatest get rich schemes, how to start up a social engineering site that will make them millions in 8 months or blink your eyes and grow rich. People who end up making money generally plan for it.

There is always an element of luck and risk and for those who are lucky in their risks their rewards can be astronomical. The other side of the coin is that their risk can be financially devastating as the recent home loan meltdown has proven. Banks and people are being punished for being greedy.

What about the rest of us?

If you have been saving money, paying off your mortgage, keeping your credit card bills down to zero or paying them off monthly, congratulations. You are on the way to for financial success. People who have money will be in a better position to scoop up realty in the current environment and make profitable investments.

There will always be some sort of opportunity to make money and as the cliché goes, opportunities are like Las Vegas casinos. If you see one that is attractive and miss it, don't fret, there will be another bright enticing one down the block.

Like the casinos, you need to have cash and the easiest way to have it ready is to have been saving for it. If you are working your way out of debt, congratulations as well. You will make it. It may take some time but planning now for getting out of debt will be a lot easier with your eyes open than closing your eyes and hoping it will go away.

Kim Greenblatt

Improving Communications in Business and Customer Service

Friday, August 29, 2008, 10:09:21 PM | admin

If business communication is good within a company, the chances are that the communications will be good from the customer service representatives and the public. Good communication skills equal good business rapport and more sales and less problems afterwards.

Schools need to emphasize communication more. Companies need to get their staff trained so that they will take ownership of a problem and follow through with it. Because of global communications and markets, it is not uncommon to be placed on hold where you are living in the United States and the customer service help center is in India or the Philippines. I recently had some problems trying to find out how a business handles certain problems and the customer service clerk didn't have an answer.

When I asked to speak to her supervisor she said that she wasn't in. I wondered if the rep was working from home. When I asked what else I could do to get an answer I was met with silence.

88

Sorry folks, this doesn't work for me.

Like a lot of people, I purchase goods or services sometimes with warranties. If something is under warranty, it needs to be taken care of. If there is a payment being processed I want to know how or why a payment gets handled. If the money isn't applied a certain way, why?

Take note international companies! You better start having a more efficient problem resolution service or people won't do business with you.

My guess is the problem starts with the board of directors and works down. If the Chairman of the Board doesn't care how is company responds to customers, why should his staff? If the Chairman of the board just pays lip service and doesn't implement his changes, it isn't the fault of the rank and file people.

Just a reminder again here in the United States (and to my international readers) to vote with your wallets and purses. If you are not getting the service or use of the product you are buying - don't buy the goods or services anymore.

Kim Greenblatt

Use your Sunday for Rest and Planning for the Week.

Saturday, August 30, 2008, 10:13:44 PM | admin

Sunday is traditionally a day of rest and like most of us, I find on Sundays that I end working just as hard on house chores or things that I couldn't get done during the week. One of the things I do is try to get a pulse for what is coming up in the upcoming week.

I check my calendars, reflect about what projects (if any) are hitting their deadlines, who do I need to contact to get things done, etc. I make a list of chores that have to be done and any pre-planning. An example of pre-planning is making a tickler in Outlook or a memo somewhere that quarterly taxes will be coming due and I have to write checks for the Fed and State of California. I often talk about the importance of making quarterly tax payments and if you haven't heard enough from me on the subject before, consider this your reminder. Don't forget quarterly taxes are due Sept 15 for the Fed and if you live in a state that has state income taxes, you will need to mail in a payment before that date as well to avoid possible penalties.

Fall is usually birthday and anniversary city for me. I have to start earmarking savings for birthday presents for my mother (Happy Birthday Mom!), wife (Happy Birthday Sharren) and daughter (Happy Birthday Arianna). Sure, you don't have to spend money to have a fun and profitable birthday but even if I were to prepare meals at home for the birthday people I still need to buy groceries.

If you are planning any trips, make sure your out of town resources like hotels and transportation are in place with reservations and tickets. It doesn't hurt to confirm them once before leaving. Weather changes may influence travel.

If people are coming into town, plan your time accordingly and make sure that you schedule rest time for yourself.

If you are teaching and resuming school or starting up, try and get some extra lesson plans finished in advance to give yourself some breathing space.

Interested in more suggestions? Please let me know. Otherwise I am going to actually try and REST this Sunday!

Kim Greenblatt

September Tax and Financial Planning

Sunday, August 31, 2008, 10:17:12 PM | admin

Here it is folks, we are in the last quarter of the year. For this year, we are looking at a Presidential election, possibly some important elections for you locally in your city or state and time to plan for your taxes if you haven't been doing it now.

If you haven't planned for your quarterly taxes and you owe money, get ready to write a check. Unless you are unemployed and strapped for cash, it is better to pay what you owe now rather than to risk penalties and problems later on. If you are uncertain, please check with your local tax professional.

Any donations for charity have to be taken care of in the remaining quarter of the year. Make sure that you are aware of the changes in the law for charitable contributions. If you need to get letters of appraisal big ticket items that you are donating, make sure the people that are preparing the estimates are experts in their fields. If the receiving charity doesn't use or resell your gift you may not get value for that contribution. Make sure that you understand the new contribution laws very clearly.

Planning on having children and are married? The kids will be deductions for the current year even if they are born on Dec 31 at 11:59 PM. Congratulations. Don't go out of your way to get pregnant though just for the sake of having kids. Make sure you and your spouse talk things over.

While you are it, take some time and talk about possible joint incomes if you are getting serious with your BBF or significant other and thinking about marriage.

If you are in business, take some time to see what needs pruning financially. We are in a slow business cycle and the chances are that things will get worse or stay flat before they get better.

If you are planning on buying things for investment purposes or selling them, maybe alleged collectible items, you may want to keep detailed records of your transactions. Remember too that cash is king in hard times.

Perhaps you may want to invest in a book on certain types of gambling? Part of the proceeds of all the book sales go to research Rett Syndrome (RTT). Rett Syndrome affects a girl born every fifteen minutes. Boys born with the Rett gene die at birth.

May your autumn be a profitable one and not a Fall.

Kim Greenblatt

Thinking About Filing Statuses for Taxes

Tuesday, September 02, 2008, 10:07:35 PM | admin

I received an email asking me what filing status should the person file under and I had to explain that without knowing all the background information I can't make a good determination. I am starting up teaching basic tax preparation again so I thought I would share some of my information with you, gentle profit oriented readers.

The IRS (Google them, you will find them, trust me), has more detail than you probably are interested in on the subject but let me try and bring the key points home here:

There are five filing statuses:

Single, Married Filing Jointly, Married Filing Separately, Head of Household, and Qualifying Widow(er) With Dependent Child.

If more than one filing status applies to you, choose the one that will give you the lowest tax.

Marital Status

In general, your filing status depends on whether you are considered unmarried or married. For federal tax purposes, a marriage means only a legal union between a man and a woman as husband and wife.

Unmarried persons. You are considered unmarried for the whole year if, on the last day of your tax year, you are unmarried or legally separated from your spouse under a divorce or separate maintenance decree.

State law governs whether you are married or legally separated under a divorce or separate maintenance decree.

Divorced persons. If you are divorced under a final decree by the last day of the year, you are considered unmarried for the whole year.

Divorce and remarriage. If you obtain a divorce in one year for the sole purpose of filing tax returns as unmarried individuals, and at the time of divorce you intended to and did remarry each other in the next tax year, you and your spouse must file as married individuals.

Annulled marriages. If you obtain a court decree of annulment, which holds that no valid marriage ever existed, you are considered unmarried even if you filed joint returns for earlier years. You must file amended returns (Form 1040X) claiming single or head of household status for all tax years affected by the annulment that are not closed by the statute of limitations for filing a tax return. The statute of limitations generally does not expire until 3 years after your original return was filed.

Head of household or qualifying widow(er) with dependent child. If you are considered unmarried, you may be able to file as a head of household or as a qualifying widow(er) with a dependent child. See Head of Household and Qualifying Widow(er) With Dependent Child to see if you qualify.

Married persons. If you are considered married for the whole year, you and your spouse can file a joint return, or you can file separate returns.

Considered married. You are considered married for the whole year if on the last day of your tax year you and your spouse meet any one of the following tests.
You are married and living together as husband and wife.

You are living together in a common law marriage that is recognized in the state where you now live or in the state where the common law marriage began.

You are married and living apart, but not legally separated under a decree of divorce or separate maintenance.

You are separated under an interlocutory (not final) decree of divorce. For purposes of filing a joint return, you are not considered divorced.
Spouse died during the year. If your spouse died during the year, you are considered married for the whole year for filing status purposes.

If you did not remarry before the end of the tax year, you can file a joint return for yourself and your deceased spouse. For the next 2 years, you may be entitled to the special benefits described later under Qualifying Widow(er) With Dependent Child.

If you remarried before the end of the tax year, you can file a joint return with your new spouse. Your deceased spouse's filing status is married filing separately for that year.

Married persons living apart. If you live apart from your spouse and meet certain tests, you may be considered unmarried. If this applies to you, you can file as head of household even though you are not divorced or legally separated. If you qualify to file as head of household instead of as married filing separately, your standard deduction will be

higher. Also, your tax may be lower, and you may be able to
claim the earned income credit. See Head of Household, later.

Single
Your filing status is single if, on the last day of the year, you
are unmarried or legally separated from your spouse under a
divorce or separate maintenance decree, and you do not
qualify for another filing status. To determine your marital
status on the last day of the year, see Marital Status, earlier.

Widow(er).   Your filing status may be single if you were
widowed before January 1, 2007, and did not remarry before
the end of 2007. However, you might be able to use another
filing status that will give you a lower tax. See Head of
Household and Qualifying Widow(er) With Dependent Child,
later, to see if you qualify.

How to file.   You can file Form 1040EZ (if you have no
dependents, are under 65 and not blind, and meet other
requirements), Form 1040A, or Form 1040. If you file Form
1040A or Form 1040, show your filing status as single by
checking the box on line 1. Use the Single column of the Tax
Table, or Section A of the Tax Computation Worksheet, to
figure your tax.

Married Filing Jointly
You can choose married filing jointly as your filing status if
you are married and both you and your spouse agree to file a
joint return. On a joint return, you report your combined
income and deduct your combined allowable expenses. You
can file a joint return even if one of you had no income or
deductions.

If you and your spouse decide to file a joint return, your tax
may be lower than your combined tax for the other filing
statuses. Also, your standard deduction (if you do not itemize
deductions) may be higher, and you may qualify for tax
benefits that do not apply to other filing statuses.

***

For more information, you can check with the IRS and you may be interested in checking out my book,

"Bad Tax Idea, Good Tax Idea" for some tips that accountants and tax professionals might not give you. You can find that book on Amazon (you can Google to find that too). All information posted here is for you to review and for more serious study and tax preparation, kindly due your own research or consult your tax pro!

Good luck with your thoughts on Filing Statuses for Taxes!

Kim Greenblatt

Innocent Spouse Relief Fed and State

Wednesday, September 03, 2008, 10:09:20 PM | admin

I was emailed a question about Innocent Spouse Relief. This is different from Injured Spouse relief. Information from the IRS can be found in Publication 971. The IRS has the forms and publications you need to research there, or consult with your tax pro. A quick and dirty way to get to the document is here. As I pointed out to my reader, if you are in doubt as to whether you qualify for the Innocent Spouse situation, search and follow the flow chart that is in the document. It is pretty thorough for determining if you are an Innocent Spouse or not.

For those of you living in California, you may want to check out the Franchise Tax Board as well.

They have very clear instructions as to the definition as stated below:

Who is an innocent spouse and how can I get relief of tax?
Who is an Innocent Spouse?
Generally, when a joint tax return is filed, each spouse is equally liable for all the tax, penalties, and interest for the particular joint tax year. This means the entire amount of tax,

penalties, and interest may be collected from either spouse, even if only one spouse earned all of the income.

If certain legal requirements are met, a spouse may be fully or partially relieved of the joint tax, penalties, and interest. Six categories of relief are available:

Complete or partial innocent spouse relief.
Relief by separate allocation of liability.
Equitable relief.
Relief from community income.
Relief by court order.
Relief from the tax due amount on return(s) that have been filed.
Please see the following questions and answers for more information.

Under what conditions is innocent spouse relief granted?
To qualify for innocent spouse relief, you must meet all of the following conditions:

You filed a valid, joint tax return.
You are able to prove that when you signed the return, you did not know, or have reason to believe, the liability would not be paid when the tax return was filed, or, at the time you signed the return, you did not have knowledge of the items that resulted in an audit assessment of additional tax.
The liability is attributable to your spouse.
Taking into account all of the facts and circumstances, it would be unfair to hold you liable for the tax.
Under what conditions is relief by separate allocation of liability granted?
Under this type of relief, we determine which spouse is responsible for the tax, penalties, and interest resulting from an audit of a joint return, and assign the liabilities to the responsible spouse. To qualify for this type of relief, you must have filed a joint return and show all of the following:

You were divorced, legally separated, or lived apart for 12 months prior to making your request for relief.

The tax resulting from the audit is attributable to your spouse.
You had no knowledge of the item(s) that resulted in the tax.
You did not receive a direct tax benefit.
You made your request within the applicable statute of
limitations, and not later than the date that is two years after
the date the Franchise Tax Board has begun collection
activities against you.
Under what conditions is equitable relief allowed?
If you filed a joint return, and you do not qualify for traditional
innocent spouse or separate allocation of liability relief, you
may still be considered for equitable relief from tax that results
from an audit or the underpayment of tax on your return. The
following are some of the factors considered:

Your current marital status.
Whether you experienced spousal abuse during your marriage.
Whether you had a reasonable belief at the time that you
signed the return that the tax was going to be paid; or, in the
case of tax resulting from an audit, whether you had
knowledge or reason to know of the understatement of tax.
Your current financial situation and your ability to pay the tax
liability.
Whose legal obligation it is to pay the tax liability pursuant to
a divorce decree or agreement to pay the liability.
Whether the liability is attributable to you or your spouse.
Whether you received a significant benefit from the
understatement or erroneous items that gave rise to the
liability.
Your compliance with income tax laws in later tax years.
Under what conditions is relief from community income
allowed?
You may be entitled to relief from your failure to include
community income on your separate return, if all the following
conditions are met:

You did not file a joint return.
You did not include an item of community income on your
separate return for that taxable year.
You did not know of, and had no reason to know of, that item

of community income.
The unreported income was attributable to your spouse.
Under what conditions is relief by court order allowed?
You may qualify for relief by court order if:

You have obtained a divorce from your spouse, and the court
issued an order relieving you of the unpaid tax due from a
joint liability.
You are in the process of obtaining a divorce and your joint
gross income exceeds $150,000 or you owe more then $7,500
for the tax year(s) for which you are seeking relief, send us a
letter requesting a Tax Revision Clearance Certificate, which
you will provide to the court. After the court issues its order,
you will need to provide us with a copy of the court order and
we will determine the amount of your relief. In your letter
requesting a Tax Revision Clearance Certificate be sure to
include your name, address, telephone number, and social
security number.
However, please note that the court is limited in the relief that
it can provide. The court cannot:

Relieve you of your responsibility to pay tax on your own
income.
Provide relief on taxes already paid.
Under what conditions is relief from return tax allowed?
You may be entitled to relief if you filed a joint return and the
tax liability is not fully paid, and you show that you had no
knowledge, or reason to know, of the non-payment. You must
pay the tax on your own income, and you are not entitled to
relief on taxes already paid.

Can both spouses request relief?
Yes. To request individual relief, each spouse must file an
Innocent Spouse Relief Application (FTB 705).

What will I need to provide with my innocent spouse request?
Generally, we will request that you provide the following
documents:

Your statement explaining why you believe you qualify for
relief and any documentation that supports your position.
Include your name, social security number, and the tax years
for which you are requesting relief.
Complete copies of your state and federal tax returns for the
years you are requesting relief.
If you have requested relief from the Internal Revenue Service
(IRS), please attach a copy of any IRS correspondence
responding to your request for relief.
If you are divorced, please attach a complete copy of your
divorce decree/marital settlement agreement.
You may request additional documentation based on your
specific circumstances.

Am I eligible for innocent spouse relief if I did not sign the joint
return?
No. If you did not sign the joint tax return, or we determine the
signature on the return is not yours, the joint return is invalid
and you are not eligible for innocent spouse relief. You may be
held liable for your separate tax liability based on your
separate income plus your share of any community income.

My divorce decree states my ex-spouse is responsible for the
tax liability. Am I already qualified for innocent spouse relief?
No, the decree is not sufficient to qualify you for innocent
spouse relief. But, you may qualify for Court Ordered Relief. To
qualify for Court Ordered Relief, the following items must be
included in your divorce decree/marital settlement agreement:

A specific reference to California state income tax.
The specific tax years for which you are requesting relief.
The amount or percentage of the total tax liability each
taxpayer is responsible for paying.
If you are in the process of obtaining a divorce, please contact
this department as soon as possible. We will evaluate your
case and advise you regarding the information that needs to
be included in your divorce decree or marital settlement
agreement. In some cases, you may be required to file a Tax
Revision Clearance Certificate with the court. Please note, you

will only be relieved of the liability resulting from income that you did not earn, manage, or control. See question 19 for contact information.

Do I have to be divorced to qualify for Innocent Spouse relief?
Not necessarily. For an allocation of liabilities between joint filers, you must be divorced, legally separated from the other party to the joint return, or not living together for the 12-months prior to submitting your request for relief. For Equitable Relief, the fact that a requesting spouse is divorced or legally separated is regarded as a positive factor in determining whether to grant relief.

I received Innocent Spouse Relief from the IRS. Will the Franchise Tax Board automatically grant me relief?
No. You must send us an Innocent Spouse Relief Application (FTB 705), a copy of the IRS determination letter, and a copy of your divorce decree/marital settlement agreement (if applicable). If the IRS granted you relief, we are required to allow similar relief from the state liability, if certain requirements are met.

My refund was applied against my spouse's liability. Can I file for injured spouse relief?
No. Injured spouse relief is different from innocent spouse relief. An injured spouse situation occurs when a joint tax refund is applied to the separate liability of one of the spouses who filed the joint return, such as past due separate tax liabilities or child support. California law does not have an injured spouse relief provision.

Will the FTB notify my spouse of my request for relief from a joint tax liability?
Yes. We are legally required to notify your spouse (or former spouse) and to allow the non-requesting spouse an opportunity to provide documentation to show why you should or should not be granted relief. We will also notify your spouse of our action on your request and provide the non-requesting spouse with an opportunity to appeal our decision. Upon your

request, we will not disclose any of your confidential information, such as your new name and address.

I have a financial hardship and cannot pay my joint tax liability. Do I qualify for innocent spouse relief based on my financial situation?
No. A financial hardship alone does not entitle you to innocent spouse relief. However, your inability to make payment may be a factor considered for granting you equitable relief.

Will the FTB delay collection action if I decide to request relief?
Generally, upon receipt of your written request for relief, all collection activity against you will be suspended. However, interest will continue to accrue while your request is being reviewed.

Will I receive a refund if I am granted relief?
If relief is granted, under certain circumstances, a refund of amounts that you have paid may be allowed.

How do I request Innocent Spouse relief?
File an Innocent Spouse Application and attach a written statement explaining why you feel you qualify for relief. You can download the application from our Website, or we will mail one to you upon request. Call (916) 845-7072 (Monday thru Friday 8 am-5pm), or write to us at:

Franchise Tax Board MS A-452
Innocent Spouse Program
PO Box 2966
Rancho Cordova 95741-2966

Assistance in Spanish is also available.

If you have any additional questions, you can call the Innocent Spouse Program at (916) 845-7072 to discuss your specific case and circumstances.

Will you deny me relief if I do not provide the information you request?

We will base our decision on all of the information available to us. It is very important that you provide us with any information you have that supports your request for relief. We cannot act favorably on your request if we do not have enough information to conclude that you are entitled to relief.

Where can I get more information on the IRS Innocent Spouse Program?
Refer to IRS Tax Information for Innocent Spouses

****

Again, this is different than being an Injured Spouse and I will try and blog on that next.
Consult your favorite tax professional and as always, since you are the one signing the tax returns, please do your own due diligence.

Kim Greenblatt

Injured Spouse

Thursday, September 04, 2008, 10:08:18 PM | admin

You are considered an Injured Spouse (not to be confused with an Innocent Spouse), if you are filing a joint tax return with your spouse and all of a sudden instead of getting the refund you were anticipating you find out that your handsome husband (or lovely wife) owes back taxes, child support, student loan payments - you get the idea.

Publication 8379 has the definition and the form is there for you to determine yourself if you can get back YOUR portion of the tax refund that you have calculated. If there is money from your spouse that he or she was suppose to get back, that will go towards whatever it is that they are trying to pay off.

If you are a California resident, sorry, California does not have the Injured Spouse relief provision. Remember my motto, please consult your own tax professional to see how this affects your situation!

I've dealt with Injured and Innocent Spouse Relief and some free advice here is that you need to make sure that your paperwork and financial dealings are clear, properly dated and separate. Questions that will be asked are on the reasonableness of the claim.

At the state level, a lot of the claims may not fly because remember, in some states, and California is one of them, property is treated as community property. That means, dear readers, it is split fifty-fifty. The love, the income and the debt!

That can make for some sticky dealings in a marriage so make sure if you are thinking of getting married that you talk <u>money</u> issues out to prevent them from surfacing later.

Kim Greenblatt

I hope you have gotten at least one bit of information, suggestion or glimmer of wisdom from the book. These are trying times for all of us and it is important that we do what we can to protect our loved ones, our friends and ourselves. Good luck!
Interested in more information?

I can be found at <u>http://www.kimgreenblatt.com</u>

I can also be contacted at <u>kimg@kimgreenblatt.com</u>

The email address may change so check my website or blog for more information.

My blog, profitable, can be read at:

<u>http://www.kimgreenblatt.com/wordpress</u>

I write about business, dealing with special needs, taxes, marketing, poker, gambling and saving money. I also have a fiction line of books through Shockingly Awesome Press at:

<u>http://www.shockinglyawesome.com</u>

I look forward to helping you grow financially!

Part of the proceeds from the sales of this book goes to research for finding a cure for Rett Syndrome. Rett Syndrome affects one girl born on the planet every fifteen minutes. Boys with the Rett gene usually die at birth.

Good luck with your financial planning and you are in my thoughts and prayers!